PRAISE FOR

LEADERSHIP SHOCK
AND PETE STEINBERG

"Working with Pete when I became the CEO of Oliver Wyman was great. The Authentic Leadership Model helped me think more clearly about where I wanted to focus my time and what sort of leader I wanted to be. Any leader going through a leadership transition would find this book a strong guiding hand towards impactful leadership."

–Scott McDonald
Chief Executive of the British Council

"Whether you are transitioning to becoming an Olympic Coach, or an executive getting that big promotion, *Leadership Shock* provides a path to greater success."

–Emilie Bydwell
Head Coach of the USA Women's Rugby Sevens

"*Leadership Shock* is a powerful book for any leader going through a transition."

–Geoff Tanner
President and CEO of Simply Good Foods

LEADERSHIP ⚡ SHOCK

PETE STEINBERG

LEADERSHIP SHOCK

USING AUTHENTICITY
TO NAVIGATE
THE HIDDEN DANGERS
OF CAREER SUCCESS

Advantage | Books

Published by Advantage Books, Charleston, South Carolina.
An imprint of Advantage Media.

ADVANTAGE is a registered trademark, and the Advantage colophon is a trademark of Advantage Media Group, Inc.

Printed in the United States of America.

10 9 8 7 6 5 4 3 2 1

ISBN: 978-1-64225-937-7 (Hardcover)
ISBN: 979-8-89188-070-2 (Paperback)
ISBN: 978-1-64225-936-0 (eBook)

Library of Congress Control Number: 2024900367

Cover and layout design by Matthew Morse.

This publication is designed to provide accurate and authoritative information in regard to the subject matter covered. It is sold with the understanding that the publisher is not engaged in rendering legal, accounting, or other professional services. If legal advice or other expert assistance is required, the services of a competent professional person should be sought.

Advantage Books is an imprint of Advantage Media Group. Advantage Media helps busy entrepreneurs, CEOs, and leaders write and publish a book to grow their business and become the authority in their field. Advantage authors comprise an exclusive community of industry professionals, idea-makers, and thought leaders. For more information go to **advantagemedia.com**.

This book is dedicated to my family.

*Without the support of my wife, Yvonne, and my children,
Penny and Elliot, I would not have had the experiences as a coach
to help me build the Authentic Leadership Model.*

"Daddy always comes back!"

CONTENTS

FOREWORD

Sandy Torchia is the Vice Chair of Talent and Culture at KPMG US and a current executive coaching client

When I reflect on the leaders who've consistently inspired me—whether they've handled challenges and failures with grace or managed success with a balance of celebration and humility or championed inclusion or made recognition their brand—the ones who made the biggest impression all had one thing in common: they're authentic.

In my twenty-six years at KPMG, I've had time to shape my own leadership philosophy. On a broader scale, I want to be the kind of leader to empower my team to learn and grow their skills and careers and lead the elements of the organization's strategy they're responsible for. I also believe it's imperative to establish clear expectations that when you're part of my leadership team, your responsibilities are broader than just your individual role.

It's a blend of giving colleagues the opportunity to make sound decisions, while I provide guidance and the tools they need to successfully do their jobs, bring the right people in, create teams that truly enjoy working together, plus get involved when they need me, all while doing it authentically.

It is an ambitious undertaking for sure, and Pete is helping me with it.

I first met Pete in the winter of 2022 while I was interviewing for my current role as the firm's vice chair of talent and culture (T&C). He was asked by our CEO to assess each candidate's leadership style against the success profile for the job, but I was also familiar with his work as an executive coach.

Even though I'd been at KPMG for two and a half decades before starting this new role, I lacked prior experience in the field of human resources, and it was also the most senior leadership position I'd ever held. So when I was selected, it was important to me, and to my own bosses, too, to engage with a leadership coach who had the knowledge and expertise in human resources, plus who could help me evolve my leadership style.

Honestly, it was foundational for me to have Pete as my coach—I knew my chances of being successful would be better if I had him at my side.

Pete's framework, whether you're starting a bigger job or working in a space that's unfamiliar to you or a combination of both, asks you to reflect on your purpose, strengths, and approach so you can truly lean in to being an authentic leader, all while making important adjustments to your priorities and style where you need to—and hopefully avoid that "leadership shock" so many experience.

As we did the work, I was able to tap into my leadership philosophy to clearly articulate the kind of leader I want to be. Pete and I defined my purpose as leading T&C to tackle big challenges, all while having fun along the way. I also want to bring value by removing any barriers so team members can effectively and successfully get their work done.

However, as we better understood my purpose, strengths, and approach, some key hurdles to achieving that came to light that I think many leaders can relate to—issues with time management, getting too into the weeds, and often relying on what worked in the past.

We got right to work tackling these challenges, starting first with my overbooked calendar. How could I start to prioritize my time to think strategically or pay attention to what mattered most when I was in back-to-back meetings all day? After many discussions with Pete about what was most important to me and to the firm, plus the difference between management and leadership, he helped me see the ways I could better focus my time.

The second item we looked at together—which to be honest also had a lot to do with my busy calendar—was my passion for diving deep into the details. I'd always been inclined to be super immersed in my learnings, especially when I was leading in an area that was new to me.

But with Pete's help I realized I was more acutely involved in the inner workings of most projects than I probably should've been, and thankfully because I was brand new to human resources and all its various functions, I couldn't go straight into the details like I had before.

I learned that there were other ways to approach being an effective leader without forcing myself to always be the subject matter expert, namely getting to know my new team. Once I understood their strengths and capabilities, I could trust in their work, lead when and where they needed me, and step back when they didn't. All of this was key to freeing up my time and allowing me to focus where I truly needed to.

I'll confess, this wasn't an easy transition for me. Being a subject matter expert had always been a strength of mine, which is why I was inclined to jump headfirst into learning everything I could when I took on my new role. I think it's human nature to have confidence in the skills that made us successful in the past. However, what I find really appealing about Pete's approach is that he gives you the necessary tools to reorient your mindset, retaining your strengths that are relevant to your new role, while adjusting others to avoid potential challenges.

One of my strengths Pete helped me focus on, which he knew would continue to serve me well in my new role (and was truly important for me because I didn't know my new team going into the job) was building relationships.

I'd always enjoyed networking and creating connections with colleagues, leaders, and clients alike and then leveraging those relationships to help me and my teams operate more efficiently, like moving agenda items forward, giving or receiving feedback, or solving cross-organizational problems. Less than two years into the role, I can look back and see that the rapport and trust I was able to develop over time was integral to my success.

All of these shifts in my leadership approach, whether major or minor, channeled me into being a more authentic version of myself. Although I was surrounded by leaders I admired, or I learned great skills from, their style was not what worked best for me.

While being true to yourself isn't always easy to put it into practice, the long-term benefits are undeniable. I now understand how important it is as a leader to embrace my authentic self. I want to enjoy the people I work with, not to mention the work itself, and lead in a way that enables my team to experience a collective purpose, maintain a healthy balance between work and home life, and incorporate fun into the mix, too, all while advancing our firm's talent strategy.

The framework Pete offers you in *Leadership Shock*—reflecting on your purpose, strengths, and approach—is not about navigating around the challenges and "shock" you may face in the road ahead, but instead finding a way through, all by adopting your most authentic leadership style.

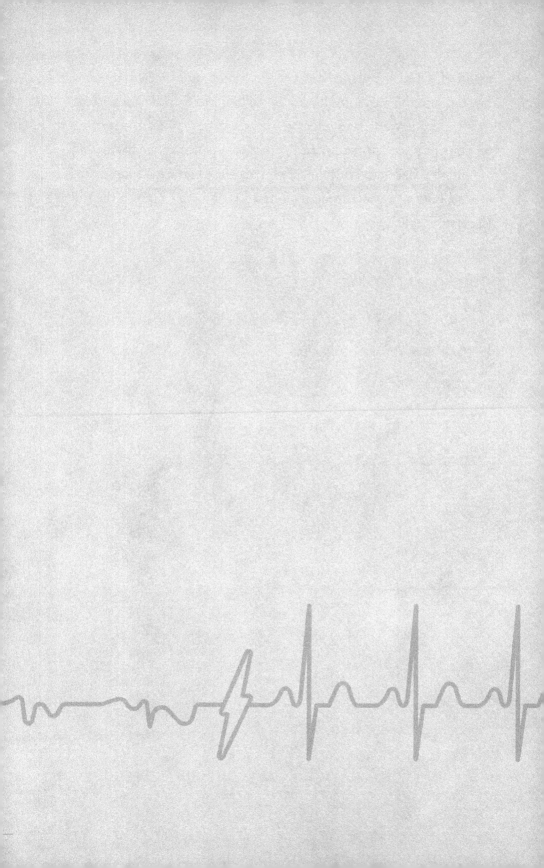

ACKNOWLEDGMENTS

As a rugby coach, I frequently reminded my players that the journey is as important as the destination. I have learned that publishing a manuscript is also a journey that, much like a rugby match, requires a team of people working together to achieve a successful result. *Leadership Shock* is in your hands today due to the support, inspiration, and guidance of people I am lucky to call family, friends, and colleagues. I am deeply grateful to all those who have played a part in making this book a reality.

First and foremost, I want to express my love and gratitude to my family. Yvonne, your patience, love, support, and ability to juggle all that you do for our family is nothing short of remarkable. Did I mention your patience? I am so proud of the family we have created together. I love you.

Penny and Elliot, "coaching" you to become the best versions of whoever you each decide to be has been the most humbling and joyful experience of my life. Mummy and Daddy love you very much.

To all the rugby players and coaches whom I have worked with, thank you for helping me develop as a coach and as a person. To all my executive coaching clients, thank you for letting me work with you and hone my craft.

To Geoff Tanner, thank you for being my first client for the Authentic Leadership Model and helping me build and enhance it.

To Sandy Torchia, thank you for being such an engaged client and sharing your experience in the opening words to introduce my work.

To Jonathan Gifford from Gifford Creative, who transformed my words into a polished manuscript, thank you for your expertise, feedback, and kindness.

To Sarah Dunbar, Kristen Miller, The Purpose Collective Team, Forbes Books, and Chris Brandt for managing the seemingly unending logistics of getting a book to print and in as many hands as possible.

I am indebted to my friends and colleagues who provided valuable insights, personal stories, feedback, and encouragement throughout this process.

To Maria Taylor, Nicky Dingemans, Corey Muñoz, and Mark Griffin, thank you for sharing your time and your thoughts with me and now my readers.

To Paul Kononoff and Nicole Massey, thank you for sharing your stories so that others may learn from them.

To the readers, as I mention in the book, I know that your time is valuable and limited. It is my hope that this book provides you with the insights, inspiration, and confidence needed to optimize your trajectory.

Lastly, I want to acknowledge the power of resilience, self-awareness, and leaders who want to better themselves, the workplace, and the world. This book is a testament to the idea that if a leader is metacognitive they will be intentional about where and how they spend their time.

ACKNOWLEDGMENTS

Thank you to everyone who has been a part of this journey. Your support has been invaluable, and I am forever grateful.

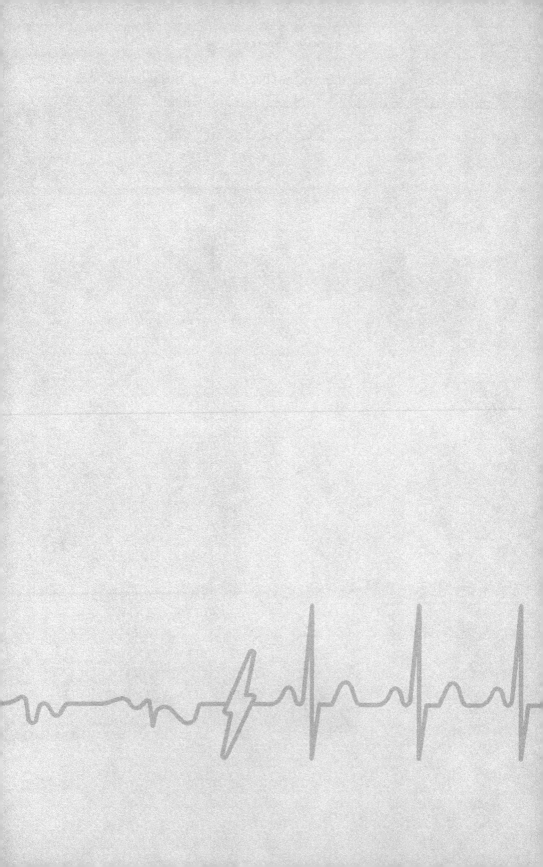

CHAPTER 1

LEADERSHIP SHOCK

A few years ago, I was running a leadership workshop at the office of one of my clients, a medium-size global pharmaceutical company.

The workshop went well. As I was chatting to people at the end of the morning, the CEO's chief of staff, Alicia, who had been at the workshop, pulled me to one side. She told me how much she had enjoyed the morning, which is always gratifying, and then she said, "Can I ask you a question? Have you worked with a leader whose calendar is fully booked? It's Michael's calendar," she explained. "It's booked solid."

Michael was the CEO of the company. He'd been promoted to the role about one year earlier. I had met him, but we hadn't actually worked together at that point. I wasn't sure what Alicia meant.

"You mean he's really busy?" I asked, stupidly.

"Well, yes. But I mean he literally doesn't have any time in his calendar. If you look at his calendar, it's booked for six full months. We have meetings we need to schedule and we're looking at the back end of the year before we can even get started. Have you come across that before?"

I began to realize what Alicia was telling me.

"I have come across that problem before," I said, "and I'm pretty sure I know what's causing it and that I can help. Would you like me to talk to Michael?"

"I'd be grateful," said Alicia. "To be honest …."

She glanced around and lowered her voice.

"To be honest, if things carry on as they are, I think Michael will kill himself with overwork, and it's kinda my job to stop that happening, you know?"

She looked at me and smiled wryly.

"But it's also not good," Alicia confided. "Things are not running well."

She broke off and looked as if she was worried she had said too much.

"Can you arrange for Michael and I to have a conversation?" I asked. "Then he can decide if he'd like to work with me on this."

"I'll look at his calendar," Alicia said without thinking.

"Good luck with that," I said, smiling.

Alicia laughed.

"Leave it with me," she said. "This is top priority."

Over the course of my career as an executive coach, I have come to recognize an overfull calendar as a classic symptom of a very particular leadership problem.

There are usually some other symptoms that go along with the calendar issue. It often becomes clear that the leader is not engaging well with the team. He or she may well be having regular meetings with key members of the team, but those key members don't seem to be getting any clear sense of direction. The leaders themselves feel overwhelmed and stressed out. They feel that they are not doing a good job and are not really on top of things. They seem to be constantly firefighting and getting tied up with issues that demand their time and attention, but they are not really moving the organization forward in the way they had planned.

Behind all this is often a sense of bewilderment. Things have always gone so well for them before. You don't get to be appointed to a senior leadership role if you don't have a track record as a successful operator. But the old tricks don't seem to be working. Something seems to have come off the rails.

I call it leadership shock. I'll tell you a lot more about it in a moment, because it is the subject of this book. First, let me tell you a bit more about Michael.

Michael had recently been promoted to CEO from his previous role as COO. Before that, he had been head of marketing for the same company. Michael was pretty much a company man.

I learned that he had been widely tipped as the strongest contender for the CEO role. The organization had interviewed several other applicants, both internal and external, and he had faced some stiff competition, but his appointment was no surprise to anyone in the company or in the wider industry and was widely welcomed.

Michael was "a safe pair of hands." He was well liked and well respected. He knew the direction he wanted to take the company, and he knew what he hoped to achieve during his time as CEO. Everything should have been plain sailing.

Instead, it was clear that Michael was struggling. On the face of it, his problem was simple: he was drowning under his workload. His calendar seemed to be out of control. But I had seen too many leaders in similar circumstances to believe that the problem was simply about Michael's calendar.

Alicia talked to Michael's assistant, Janet, and came back to me with a date for a meeting with Michael. She also gave me some more background detail.

Michael clearly wasn't finding any time for his family or any kind of social life, but he seemed to accept that as an inevitable aspect of the new role. Alicia told me that Michael was experiencing the "constantly firefighting" issue and that he wasn't able to devote the time he wanted to his big ideas—the things he most wanted to make happen during his tenure.

Alicia also hinted at tensions within the senior team. Michael was in the process of interviewing internal and external candidates for his replacement as COO. The vice president of sales took every opportunity to complain to Michael about the chief marketing officer and the chief finance officer, and was clearly getting under everyone's skin. People were turning to the CFO, Jimena, for advice and guidance—and even for decisions—because everyone was finding it hard to get any of Michael's time and attention. There was a sense of infighting and a lack of direction.

The fact that Alicia was prepared to confide so much in me was significant of itself. She was clearly anxious. Although her immediate concern was the state of Michael's calendar and the potential effect on Michael's well-being, it seemed clear to me that she could sense that something was not right in the company. Alicia had her finger firmly on the pulse of the organization, and she didn't like what she was feeling.

I have been working in the field of organizational development, leadership, innovation, and strategic planning for some twenty years now.

For many years after I started working in the corporate space, I was also an elite rugby coach. I coached the USA Women's Rugby team for two Rugby World Cups and for the Rio Olympics. I spent nineteen years as head coach for Penn State's women's rugby team, winning ten national championships.

I know a lot about the difference between success and failure. I know how to help top athletes and top executives deliver the best performance they are capable of. I have also learned a lot about what it takes for people to become highly effective leaders and about the things that cause leaders to fail.

It has taken all that knowledge and all that experience for me to recognize something that has probably been staring me in the face for much of that time: that a great many executives fail not because of some defect they have (and least of all because of some mistake they make; everyone makes mistakes) but because they have gone into a form of leadership shock.

Leadership shock can happen at any stage in a leader's career.

It is generally less serious when it happens early in someone's career. When people take on a leadership role for the first time in their lives, they are acutely aware of the new challenges they face. They are looking out for signs that something might be going wrong because they know they are in a new kind of role and that different things will be expected from them. They realize that their behavior is going to need to change.

They may be experiencing a degree of leadership shock, but at least they are expecting it. And because they are aware they are in uncharted territory and that there are risks and dangers ahead, there is a good chance they will adapt and survive. They are usually keen to learn more and are open to advice and guidance. The main threat for new leaders is that high-quality advice may not be made available to them and, if so, they may fail to seek out good advice in their early days.

Experienced leaders face a different problem. The leadership principles and behaviors they have developed over the years have proven successful—by definition. Those principles and behaviors are pretty much ingrained by now, and, in any case, it often doesn't occur to the leader that their new role may require them to draw on different aspects of their leadership strengths or develop new ways of working with colleagues. Everything has worked perfectly up until now, so why change?

It is often especially hard to see the need for change when leaders take up a new, more senior role in the same organization. In a different organization, they are more alert to the possibility that change will be needed: there will likely be a different culture and different expectations of how leaders should behave. When leaders are promoted within the organization they have worked in for perhaps many years, everything seems, on the face of it, to be the same.

When leaders find that what has always worked so well for them in the past is no longer working, they literally don't know what has hit them. They can't imagine what action they can take to fix the problem. They feel as if the ground is shifting beneath their feet and that everything they believed to be true about themselves and about the world around them is suddenly in question.

What I started to realize, after I had been working as a leadership consultant for some years, was that all the leaders who were turning to me because they were facing this kind of problem with their leadership were all going through some form of transition. It might be the business environment they operated in, but more often it was a new role; a new boss; a reorganization … Something had changed that was causing the problem.

It was at that point that I began to recognize the symptoms of what I now know is leadership shock.

I call it leadership shock for a good reason—it's not stress; it's shock. A degree of stress is normal for any executive, especially when they take on a new role. But certain sets of circumstances can turn normal levels of stress into full-blown shock.

There is a physiological background to this. Our bodies react to stressful situations by producing hormones that increase our readiness for "fight or flight." We feel alert and full of energy, albeit a little tense and edgy. For this reason, stress can be productive. We can use the adrenaline flow to fuel our response to the worrying new situation.

Shock is different. Shock is not productive. When we go into shock, our bodies have gone beyond fight or flight. Our brains shut down all nonessential systems in a single-minded attempt to stay alive. We can function, but we can't perform.

The leaders I was working with were showing all the classic symptoms of shock. They were working hard—too hard, in a sense—but they didn't feel it was productive work. They were often sleeping badly and skipping meals. They had no life outside of work and their family life was under strain as a result. They would tell me how they felt overwhelmed by their new role, that despite all their efforts they didn't seem to be able to focus on the things they most wanted to achieve.

They had always coped with the challenges they had faced in the past, but this new change was different in some way. Their usual approaches and behaviors were not producing successful outcomes.

What they needed, but did not recognize, was to rethink their whole approach to leadership and change key aspects of their behavior.

That's a lot easier said than done.

MARIA TAYLOR
CHIEF LEARNING OFFICER, UNITED AIRLINES

"I think that when leaders are transferring to an external role, they give a lot more thought to what is expected and to the context. They do the research; they ask the questions. And if they're doing it successfully, they recognize the magnitude of the change. Or, if they're transferring with an executive recruiter, the recruiter will have those conversations with them and help prep them, where an internal person doesn't necessarily have those conversations.

"When you transfer internally to a larger role, everything changes, but it's in ways that are subtle. I think sometimes it can be harder. Because you know the people, you think you know the job, you think you know the context. What you don't recognize is how dramatically the context and expectations have changed—and often you don't really adapt to it. You're not thinking about it in a different and big-picture way, and you're relying on the skill set that got you there to take you forward successfully, which doesn't always work."

Do You Have Leadership Shock?

Try this short questionnaire to discover whether and to what extent you are already suffering from leadership shock. Please answer this on a 5-point scale related to your current role. Add up your score (1, 2, 3, etc.) for each response.

STRONGLY DISAGREE	DISAGREE	NEITHER AGREE NOR DISAGREE	AGREE	STRONGLY AGREE
1	2	3	4	5

QUESTIONS	SCORE
I can manage my calendar to make sure I focus on my priorities.	
My priorities are clear for my role, and I have a clear plan to be successful.	
I can lead in a way that is authentic to who I am.	
I have a clear vision that will allow me to fulfill my role effectively.	
I understand what motivates me and makes me fulfilled.	
I know the strengths that I bring to this role.	
TOTAL SCORE	

YOUR SCORE:

26–30   Congratulations, you are in great leadership health.

21–25   Beware! You are doing OK but need to monitor your leadership health.

16–20   You have mild leadership shock and it is preventing you from being successful.

1–15   You are in full leadership shock. (But don't worry—we will work together to return you to great leadership health.)

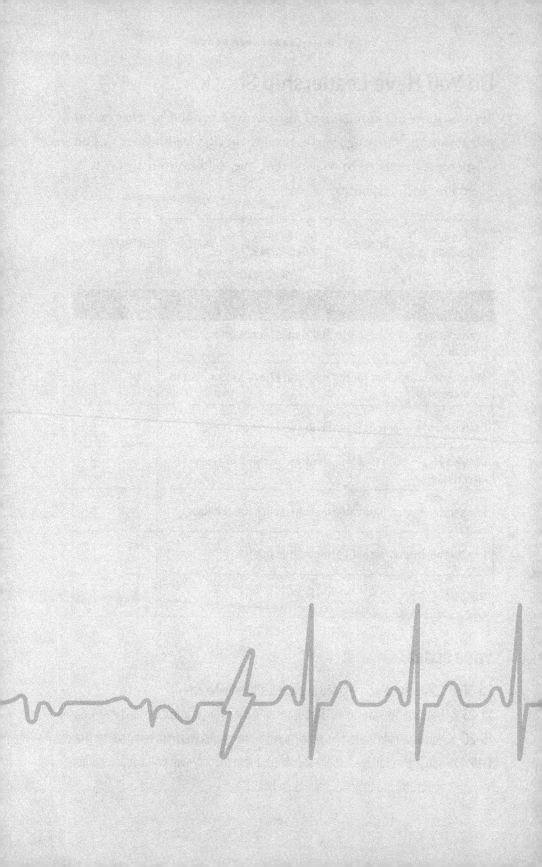

CHAPTER 2

THE AUTHENTIC LEADERSHIP MODEL

Before I became a leadership coach, I was a scientist—a geochemist, to be precise—and perhaps because of that science background, I tend to think in terms of systems. I think about how different aspects of a system interact to cause something else to happen.

I used to work on climate modeling, for example. What I like about climate modeling is that if you change one factor in any aspect of the system, you see the impact of that change somewhere else, and you can make the connections—even though they can be very complex. You can see how even a small change in one place can ripple through the whole system and sometimes have quite a dramatic effect somewhere else in the system.

That also fed into my work as a rugby coach. I felt that players needed to have a set of principles that would inform how they approached their game. Putting together a team of individually brilliant athletes isn't enough to win matches. The team needs principles that will guide the kind of moves they choose to initiate and how they respond effectively to attacks from the other side. Over time, these principles create a set of "instinctive" behaviors; the team learns to play in a winning way. You see this in all great teams: someone always seems to be in the right place at the right time; small opportunities are cleverly exploited; mistakes by the opposition are seized on ruthlessly.

All successful leaders built up a similar set of principles over time that underpin their responses to a wide variety of situations. These principles have also become "instinctive"; we stop questioning why we behave or respond in certain ways.

When leaders are in a period of transition, they need to revisit all of their assumptions and question whether these are driving the right behaviors in their new, different leadership environment.

One way of describing this is to say that leaders need to be metacognitive: they need to think about how they think. They need to question why they believe a particular action is appropriate and consider what in their past experience has led to that belief. Because it may well be that the new leadership environment demands different behaviors and that they need to develop a new set of beliefs.

When I work with executives in transition who are experiencing leadership shock, the process we go through is like a search operation. We have to search for the principles that are driving behaviors that are no longer effective. Leaders need to get to the point where they can think, "I always tended to do this in such and such a situation, because of this particular belief, approach, or guiding principle." Once they become aware of this, they can think about whether that belief or guiding principle is delivering the behaviors that are best suited to their new role.

To go back to my climate models, these leaders are experiencing a change in the weather that is having a serious impact on their ability to function successfully. Our task is to search for the factors hidden somewhere in their current leadership model that are resulting in ineffective responses that are only making things worse.

My approach to executive coaching has always been to not just try to solve the immediate issue, whatever that might be, but also to give my clients a framework that will allow them to cope with any future challenges they may face. I try to help leaders become aware of their own thought processes—the various principles and approaches that guide their behaviors and the choices they make about their own behaviors.

For most of us, these principles, approaches, choices, and behaviors tend to be unconscious or "instinctive." A better word might be *implicit*. We've adopted these principles, made these choices, and behaved in these ways over the years because they have proved effective for us. But we very often don't bring these things into the cold light of day and examine them closely. We don't make them *explicit*.

To help leaders do that, I have developed the Authentic Leadership Model.

The Authentic Leadership Model allows leaders to understand which of the expectations, strengths, principles, and choices in their leadership are driving behaviors that are no longer successful in the new environment, and it allows them to understand which aspect of their current leadership model needs to change.

It is authentic because it is based on some fundamental aspects of views and beliefs that the leader has. Perhaps most importantly, it is authentic because it helps a leader be certain that what they are doing fits with their core purpose—the thing that makes them come to work in the morning eager to get started and that fills their emotional tank.

The model is a framework that helps guide thinking, but the individual needs to flesh out that framework with their own vision, personal strengths, and individual approach to leadership.

The major benefit of this approach is that it is a long-term fix. Once we have become aware of every aspect of our own leadership model, and the metacognitive skills required, we can adapt aspects of it at any time to suit new challenges and changing conditions.

When Alicia got me my first meeting with Michael to talk about his calendar, I was already doing some team development work with the company. I talked to Michael about the Authentic Leadership Model and his first reaction was that he wanted me to work with all of his senior team on their own leadership models and to use that as a way to explore everyone's roles and responsibilities.

It was a big job. I was very excited. And then I said something pretty foolish.

"Thanks very much," I said. "I'd love to."

So far, so good.

"But I'm not prepared to do it," I went on, "unless you and I can work together to develop your own leadership model, which is quite a big commitment of your time and attention."

It was a crazy thing to say. I was risking the loss of a great deal of business, just because Michael might not be prepared to devote the time and effort to developing his own leadership model. But I knew that if Michael didn't develop his own leadership model, he would stay in leadership shock and any effort I put into developing the rest of the team's models would be wasted. Nothing would change and Michael would fail to achieve what he wanted with the business.

I tried to explain this to Michael.

"If we don't work on your own leadership model," I said, "and think about how you adapt your leadership to meet your new challenges, you won't be able to effectively implement the changes you want to make to the team's roles and responsibilities. I'm not prepared to take your money and then do a bad job for you and for the organization. If I'm going to work with the team on their leadership models, you and I have to work together on your own leadership model as well."

Or something along those lines.

Michael was quiet.

"Hm," he said finally. "Thank you. I'll have to think about it. My gut reaction is that going through this process with you is not sufficiently business focused. The company needs me to be focused on the business right now."

"The Authentic Leadership Model *is* business focused," I said. "It's about helping you focus on your vision for the business and determine your real priorities so you can leverage your strengths to achieve that vision. Your calendar is overwhelming you at the moment …."

Michael smiled wanly.

"I can help you with that—but once we have been through your leadership model you will have a clear idea of where you want to focus your time. It will be obvious to you what is essential and what you can say 'no' to and leave to somebody else."

"Sounds good!" said Michael, sounding not entirely convinced. "Give me a few days to think about it."

I smiled as bravely as I was able to and said I looked forward to hearing from him and left the office. Michael's assistant, Janet, smiled at me as I left.

And then I waited.

And waited.

Two weeks later, Michael called me himself.

"I'm sorry it's been a while," he began. "I've had to think about this a lot. And, you know, it's very hard for me to make time to do this right now. I've had to decide whether it's the right use of my time."

I swallowed hard and mumbled something like, "Ah-ha. Hm. OK."

There was silence.

"And I've decided I need to do this," Michael said finally. "I think it's important."

Mentally, I leaped out of my chair and did a victory lap around the office, high-fiving nonexistent fellow coaches and trainers. In reality, I sat tight. I said I would get in touch with Alicia to fix a schedule of meetings.

"That's great," said Michael. "Thank you."

When I spoke to Alicia about working with Janet to get some slots in Michael's calendar, she gave me an old-fashioned look because, to be fair, she and I were probably the two people on the planet who best understood what a nightmare Michael's calendar was.

She got Michael's calendar up on the screen.

"Just get me one session for now," I pleaded. "As soon as possible. Is there any meeting coming up in the next few weeks you don't think is critical?"

"Well, I'm going to have to talk to Janet, obviously, but let's have a look," said Alicia.

She scrolled through Michael's calendar, pulling a variety of interesting faces as she did so, from mild impatience to suppressed fury.

What happened next was interesting.

Alicia homed in on a monthly one-on-one session Michael had scheduled for the following week with the head of sales, a man called Jeffrey.

"That can wait," Alicia said brusquely. "Jeff will live for a month without seeing Michael."

"That will do nicely," I said, thanking her.

Now we could get started on Michael's leadership model, but first we needed to do something about his calendar.

There are a few "tricks" that I use with clients to help them get on top of their workload in the short term.

I call them tricks because they are not part of the leadership model. Once we have created an Authentic Leadership Model and we have a leader's purpose, vision, values, and all of the other elements firmly in place, then their real priorities will be clear to them and none of these tricks will be necessary. But we couldn't even begin to talk about Michael's leadership model until we had cleared a bit of space in his calendar. So, we applied a few of my tricks.

One of my favorite tricks is "the shotgun approach."

"What we're going to do today," I said to Michael and Alicia (this first meeting, at my suggestion, was with the two of them together), "is to take a shotgun to your calendar."

Michael looked skeptical; Alicia looked excited. Her eyes glinted and she smiled a tight-lipped, slightly manic smile. If I had been Michael's calendar, I would have been scared.

"We're going to block out some things in your calendar that you decide are absolutely essential—we're going to 'bulletproof' those, if you like—and then we're going to blast holes in your calendar through the bits that aren't bulletproofed."

Alicia's tight smile became even more bloodcurdling. I suspected she was mentally slotting cartridges into a virtual pump-action shotgun and putting on a pair of dark shades.

Most of us have an attitude to time that is a bit warped. Our near schedule (this week) is always crazy busy and there is very little flexibility. A leader would only add an absolutely critical meeting to this coming week. A month from now the schedule looks more open, so we often add noncritical meetings. That'll be fine, we tell ourselves. We'll have time on our hands by then. But that noncritical stuff that was booked weeks ago has now clogged up our calendar. It can actually be blasted without much damage being done.

"OK," I said, "let's start with emergencies. I assume some things in the calendar are literally firefighting … things that absolutely have to be fixed right now?"

Michael nodded.

"Let's imagine a two-by-two grid with the axes being urgent and important," I said. "In the top right-hand corner there's a large wildfire. It's ablaze—it's urgent and important. So you have to go there, right now. In the top left-hand corner, there's a small bit of grassland with flames. This is urgent but not important. So maybe you could send someone else there to check it out. Bottom right-hand corner, it's smoldering; it's smoking, but there are no flames—important but not urgent. You need to keep an eye on that. Bottom left-hand corner is a patch of land you're worried about in the longer term. You need to do a safety check on that sometime to be on the safe side. Not important and not urgent."

I could sense Michael running through a mental checklist of his own priorities.

"Let's start with your wildfires," I concluded. "'Important and urgent' first. Let's bulletproof those."

Michael immediately pointed to two major sets of meetings in the calendar. "Anything related to those has to stay in," he said, glancing at Alicia, who clearly knew exactly what Michael meant. She marked a series of meetings with a red highlighter.

Michael thought a bit longer.

"Top left-hand corner," he said. "What was that? Some flames but maybe someone else could take a look? That's harder."

He pointed Alicia to another series of meetings. "I need to stay on top of those, but I don't think they're going to have a big impact," said Michael. Alicia started to highlight another tranche of meetings in a different color.

"Bottom right," he continued. "Smoke but no fire. I don't like those. But maybe I don't absolutely have to go myself."

He mentioned a few issues to Alicia, who nodded and got to work highlighting.

"Bottom left?" I prompted. "No smoke, no fire, but safety checks?"

Michael stared off into the distance for a while. "Well, that's kind of 'everything else,'" he said finally. "It's hard to pick anything out. But I can't just leave everything and hope nothing bad happens."

"Try another trick," I suggested. "It's just another way of seeing the same thing. If you don't go to those meetings, what's the worst thing that could happen? Could it be immediately catastrophic?"

"Well, not catastrophic, no," agreed Michael. "And certainly not immediately."

"So no major potential issues in this quarter?" I suggested. "Or maybe longer? Could you bounce those meetings back by a quarter and check up on them then?"

Michael nodded at Alicia, who got to work.

"One last thing," I said. "Let's forget about firefighting or catastrophes for a moment. There are a lot of meetings that just help keep things running smoothly, or keep everyone up to speed, or which are corporate obligations: charities, industry bodies, stakeholder relationships. That kind of thing."

Michael nodded.

"Here's an idea. Think about meetings from the perspective of your role rather than you personally. You feel obliged to attend some meetings, internal and external, because of the relationship you have with people. You know … 'Jeff will want to see me; Mary will expect me to be there.' But the question is not really, 'Does Michael need to be there?' but, 'Does the CEO need to be there? Does the CEO absolutely have to do this?' And if the CEO doesn't have to be there, which senior figure could go instead? Or maybe nobody senior needs to be there at all and a designated champion of that relationship could attend and send you a quick note with the minutes and a brief summary?"

Michael and Alicia glanced at each other. I could see Alicia's mind whirring.

"For example," I continued, sensing I was on a roll, "you could delegate some things upward as well as downward. I know you have a big commitment to the company's charitable involvements and various industry bodies …"

Michael nodded again.

"They expect to see the company represented at key events. Delegating upward, could it maybe be a board member? Or even the chairman? It's important the company has a presence at these meetings and events, but it doesn't always have to be the CEO, right?"

Michael looked thoughtful.

"Can I ask …?" I ventured.

Michael looked receptive. I plowed on.

"I see you have a lot of regular 'routine' meetings with your key colleagues. For example, Alicia and Janet 'stole' one of your routines with Jeff, your head of sales, to create space for this meeting."

Alicia looked quietly triumphant.

"Are those routines always essential?" I asked.

"Well, I need to be plugged into what's going on," Michael shot back, a bit tersely. "And for them to feel that they know they have my time; that they are guaranteed regular access to me."

I nodded. I felt that Alicia glanced at me in a slightly conspiratorial way.

"It's just a thought," I said.

Over the coming weeks, Alicia and Janet began to "take a shotgun" to Michael's calendar, with some immediate benefits. They also began to deflect other meeting requests either up or down, delegating some to senior members of the team and asking the chairman, Alvin, if he could stand in for some of the more ceremonial duties.

If nothing else, the shot-up calendar helped her to schedule the ongoing weekly meetings for Michael and me to begin work on his leadership model.

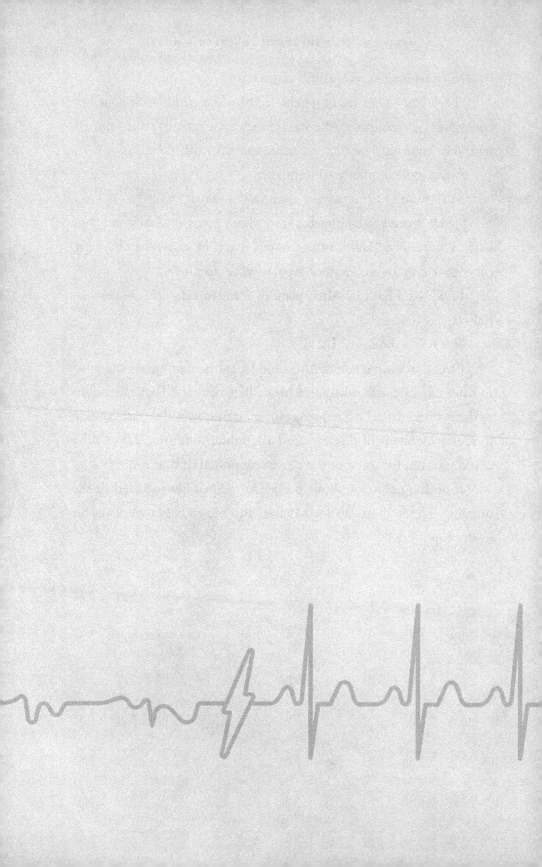

CHAPTER 3

PURPOSE

In my next meeting with Michael, we chatted about his calendar and asked if Alicia and Janet's efforts were helping. He seemed to welcome the small amount of free time it was generating for him but also seemed anxious that he might be missing out on something; that things might be beginning to go wrong that he was unaware of, or that opportunities might be slipping past him, unseen.

"You can't be everywhere all the time," I suggested.

Michael didn't look reassured.

I like to start the process of developing someone's Authentic Leadership Model by exploring what they see as their purpose: the thing that makes people feel good about themselves and gets them out of bed in the morning.

I started out with some of the questions I typically use to try to uncover a client's purpose.

"Can you tell me about what you are doing when you feel best about yourself? About when you feel most accomplished?" I asked.

Michael is a thoughtful man.

"I think those might be two different things," he replied, after a pause. "At the moment I feel best about myself when I actually manage to spend some time with my wife and family, but I know that's not what you're driving at."

"I came up through the marketing side," he went on. "I moved into product management, and I helped launch several important products; very valuable drugs; very successful. I like to think I know a lot about how this industry works."

He glanced across at me. I nodded.

"So I think perhaps when I feel most *accomplished* is when I'm using all of my skills and experience to make things happen to get a good result. The times when I am firing on all cylinders and feeling on top of my game. I feel pretty good at those times."

"Can you describe some examples of the best of those moments?"

"Oh, when we get a drug to market, obviously," he said immediately. "I get satisfaction out of putting in the effort and seeing the whole process through, passing each milestone on the way. But it's when the drug gets to patients that is the best moment. When it's out there helping people."

"That must be a good moment," I agreed. "Would you describe that as a moment of professional satisfaction—perhaps more than that; maybe professional triumph—or is it also emotional? What is happening when you feel really good about yourself ... when your emotional tank gets filled?"

"Oh, there's a very emotional component," Michael readily agreed. "It's very satisfying. You feel you've done something worthwhile. So, yes. That fills my emotional tank. That keeps me going."

"Also," he continued after a pause, "It's very much a team effort. Taking a drug from research to approval to market involves hundreds of people. Maybe thousands in all. It's a huge communal effort and it's very rewarding."

"Are there times outside the industry where you get that kind of satisfaction?" I asked. "In your hobbies or your outside activities?"

"Well, I don't really have any hobbies at the moment," Michael said, a little wistfully. "I used to play a lot of soccer and I used to coach a youth team, and I got a lot of satisfaction from that. That has had to be put aside for a while now. But I've also always been active with various charities, especially cancer charities. My wife had a brush with breast cancer. I work with our local charities on a personal basis, but one of the perks of my job is that I also get to work with charities and NGOs at a global level. So that's very satisfying."

After a bit more discussion it became clear that working with teams of people to get things done was a big part of Michael's make-up.

"I do like working with teams," he said finally. "I'm very happy working by myself but I don't believe we can achieve as much working on our own. If we're going to achieve big things, we need people's collective intelligence."

Michael's purpose was beginning to emerge quite clearly. We tried a few variations.

We explored "Working with teams to achieve results," but Michael found that too simplistic.

"I like to get results," he agreed. "But it's the big things that are really rewarding. The things that will make a difference in the world. That's why I work in the pharmaceutical industry. That's why I work with charities."

We thought more about Michael's purpose and looked at it from many angles. We settled on "Working as a team to make a difference in people's lives."

We need to know what our core purpose is before we can decide on all the other elements of our Authentic Leadership Model.

For Michael, surfacing his purpose of "Working as a team to make a difference in people's lives" would be key to helping him decide on the impact he wanted to have as CEO and how he could best bring that about.

Our purpose can sometimes seem quite straightforward, even mundane. That doesn't matter. The point is not to have the most impressive-sounding purpose but to find what it is that makes you fulfilled and satisfied. Because if you set out to do things that are at odds with that fundamental purpose, your heart—quite literally—won't be in it. You won't find the work you do fulfilling or rewarding and, most likely, you won't be successful in what you attempt. But the things that you *do* find fulfilling and satisfying will represent the place where you can have the most impact on the world, which will be your own way of "doing good."

As an example, I'd like to offer a real-life example about "purpose" from a friend of mine, Mark Griffin, who set up the charity Play Rugby USA.

Leading with Purpose:

Mark Griffin—Founding Partner, PurposeFused

Mark Griffin is a past USA National Rugby team player who set up the charity Play Rugby USA with the aim of "developing youth through rugby." The charity started life as a weekend rugby program for young homeless people in Brooklyn and grew into a national body encouraging grassroots rugby in underserved communities throughout the country. Mark grew up in the UK, and in 2015, he was awarded an MBE ("Member by Order of Excellence of the British Empire") by Her Majesty Queen Elizabeth II for his work with young people in the US. Mark is also a founding partner of the purpose-driven consultancy, PurposeFused.

Mark and I met through the world of rugby—not as players but as fellow coaches and through our involvement with USA Rugby, the sport's governing body. I nominated Mark for the sport's Hershey's STRIVE Award for his pioneering work with young people, using rugby as a way of instilling a sense of self-worth and purpose in kids growing up in pretty challenging and underprivileged environments. I'm happy to report that Mark won that award!

I talked to Mark about his ideas around purpose.

"I like to think about filling people up with purpose rather than trying to squeeze them dry," Mark said.

"If you fill people up and everybody is overflowing with energy and enthusiasm, there's an opportunity not just to get more out of each individual, but also to have people work better together, because that becomes contagious, in a good way. So my particular approach is, 'How can we use purpose as a vehicle to unlock people's potential so they can show up as the ultimate version of themselves and perform at their absolute best; to support each other in that process of performing at their best and leave whatever it is they're doing knowing that they've made an impact?'"

Mark's PurposeFused consultancy uses a formula to help define purpose: "Purpose equals passion, plus impact, plus application."

"We use the word 'passion,'" said Mark, "because this has to be very much raw, intrinsic, emotional stuff to actually truly drive people's performance. It can't just be a statement that we come up with that sounds impressive.

"So passion is: 'What do you care about? What do you believe in? What are you good at? When are you at your best? What do you want to be spending your time on in the ideal world?' And then, from a work perspective, we look at 'How can I craft my role to bring out these things that I'm really passionate about and these things I want to demonstrate impact with, on a day-to-day basis?'"

Mark talks about a certain level of vulnerability that leaders need to be comfortable with in articulating their purpose and sharing it with their colleagues.

"Purpose is a framework within which people should be able to be their best self," he says. "And that does involve some level of vulnerability.

"You've got to disconnect from the ego a little bit and peel back your identity to get to your core, which isn't always a comfortable thing to do, because it's who you are; it's what you care about; it's how you want to show up.

"To be able to lead with purpose in a sustainable way—in a way that is truly authentic—we're really going to be living with purpose as well. And that doesn't mean 100 percent of your time; it's not possible! Different challenges and things are always going on in life, it's just that it always provides a nice framework for you that has lots of flexibility within it; it just helps reconnect you to the things that matter.

"When things do go off track, purpose is a powerful tool in the resilience toolbox to be able to bounce back and come back stronger."

MARIA TAYLOR

CHIEF LEARNING OFFICER, UNITED AIRLINES

"I think understanding purpose is critical. Having individual personal purpose in what they're doing is one of the most critical things that a leader can do. I think it's one of the most overlooked. I know I see in our organization day to day, people wanting to be promoted, which is natural and understandable, but they don't always know why and how that fulfills their purpose.

"One of the biggest mistakes I see leaders doing is that they rely on getting things done themselves versus developing teams, developing leaders, and their purpose in developing a leadership pipeline and the leadership legacy. There's always an operational pull, a pull for operational performance and effectiveness that actually never goes away. But how you will achieve that changes. And if you make the change from knowing that you have to get things done, to knowing that you have to get things done through people and by building the resource team, whether it's internal or external, to get things done, and setting direction, that's really important."

Summary: Purpose

Purpose is the starting point of the Authentic Leadership Model. Identifying your purpose and thinking metacognitively about what is important to you helps ground everything that comes afterward.

Your purpose helps you focus on the things that matter most to you and keep you fulfilled. Thinking about your purpose within the model helps you identify where you should spend your time in a way that is sustainable, because it's grounded in the things that are important to you.

Discovering your purpose sounds like a difficult and lengthy process, but it doesn't have to be. I usually ask clients to reflect on when they have felt most fulfilled in their career and most satisfied and found that what they are doing gives them energy, because when you feel fulfilled and energized in this way, it's usually because what you are doing is aligned with your purpose.

These are the kinds of questions that Mark Griffin of Purpose-Fused suggested to help people identify their passions in life: "What do you care about? When are you at your best? What do you want to be spending your time on in an ideal world?" I also tend to ask people about the things they find tedious and draining, because this is usually a sure sign that whatever they are doing at those times is not aligned to their purpose, which helps narrow the field.

When you lay out all of the situations where you do or do not feel fulfilled and energized and reflect on the themes that cut across them, you can identify your purpose. A purpose can be summed up in one line or it can be bullet points. It might be something like, "My purpose is to work with teams to solve big problems and have fun." Other people think about their own purpose and the purpose within the team, the organization, and the wider community. Neither approach is right nor wrong; they are just different ways of getting to the things that are authentic to us.

Later in the model, when you come to decide on your priorities and your leadership principles, choosing things that are closely connected to what you most want to achieve and to your purpose will ensure they are powerful and sustainable.

Finding Your Purpose

Here are a few questions to ask yourself that will help you discover your own purpose.

- What are you doing when you feel at your most accomplished and best?
- When do you feel satisfied and fulfilled, as if this is the best possible use of your time?
- When do you find it easy to concentrate for long periods of time?
- When is it easy for you to lead others?
- What are you doing when you find that new ideas and solutions seem to come most easily to you?
- What fills your emotional tank?
- Identify a time when you were frustrated because you could not be your best; what could you not do that led to your frustration?

EXERCISE:

Write down as many versions of your purpose as you can think of. Play around with different ways of describing your purpose. You need to come up with more than ten to get enough new ideas.

Select the three that feel most "right" for you.

Test those three against the times you identified when you felt at your best and most accomplished.

- Do any of them capture the *reason* you felt that way?
- Do you need to *combine* or *rewrite* them?

- *Share* your purpose with people that know you well; ask them for *feedback* and if they think it fits you.

- Be wary of things that sound *noble* or *worthy* but don't *actually represent* your real purpose.

- Be prepared to *come back* to your purpose and *adjust* it as you work your way through the model; remember the Authentic Leadership Model is not a linear process.

CHAPTER 4

ROLE EXPECTATION

The next time I saw Michael was a little later than planned; a couple of our meetings had been postponed.

I walked into the anteroom of the CEO's suite of offices and Janet ushered me into Michael's office.

Michael didn't look much better. He looked tired and stressed. I smiled warmly. "Michael, hi! How's it going?"

He immediately apologized for having had to move our previous appointments. I told him it was not a problem—of course … very busy … lot going on and so on—but inside I was thinking, "If you're having to cancel our meetings, what else are you having to cancel?"

Michael got up from behind his desk and motioned me to some soft chairs in a corner of the office. There was a thermos of coffee and another of hot water and various sachets of tea set out on a sideboard, along with bottles of water.

The two of us grabbed our drinks—a black coffee for Michael, some English breakfast tea for me—and sat down facing each other at a slight angle across a low glass table. Time was precious, so I launched straight in.

"In our last meeting," I said, "we settled on a 'Purpose' for you, which was 'Working as a team to make a difference in people's lives.' Have you had a chance to reflect on that? Does it still seem right for you as your Purpose? The thing that gets you out of bed in the morning and fills your emotional tank?"

I could see Michael clearing a great deal of internal mental "stuff" to recall the detail of our conversation. After a while, he relaxed a little. There was even a glimmer of a smile.

"It's nice to be reminded of why we do what we do," he said, smiling more openly. "I'm comfortable with that. That's pretty much why I'm here!"

I smiled back.

Then, probably rashly, I plunged straight in.

"You've had to reschedule a couple of meetings," I said. "It's not a problem, obviously; my time is yours. But in our last meeting, we were quite focused on trying to clear your calendar. How's that going?"

Michael immediately tensed up. He is not someone who likes to show they are irritated, but he looked irritated.

"Uh, ah, Alicia and Janet have been doing their best to clear some space, but it's not … Uh … There's a lot happening right now."

"Of course," I said. "Let's get back to the big picture."

Michael relaxed a little.

"We talked about your overarching purpose last time. Now I'd like to talk about your role as CEO. What would you say are the key expectations of your role?"

Michael looked at me a little quizzically.

"That's a huge question, obviously," I said. "But can we reflect on that? What do you feel are the key expectations of your role? I don't mean what is expected from you personally—that's more about your core strengths and how you can best leverage those. We'll come to that a bit later. I mean, what do you think are the organization's key expectations for its CEO?"

"Well, there's a set of numbers I'm supposed to deliver, and I need to keep the shareholders happy," said Michael, a little impatiently. "I think the first expectation of any CEO is to deliver the expected performance. But I don't see my main role as delivering numbers; I see it more as ensuring that the company thrives, in a far broader sense …."

"I don't want to be a complete pain in the neck," I interrupted.

Michael looked at me as if he thought I was a complete pain in the neck.

"Your vision for the role is hugely important, obviously, but a slightly different issue that I'd like to come to next, if I may. Can we stick for the moment with what you think are the board's key expectations of the CEO role?"

Michael looked cheated. Which was fair, because it's a lot more exciting to talk about your vision as a leader than it is to talk about the current expectations of the role. But it's also important to make sure we have a clear-eyed view of what is expected from us. Many successful careers have foundered because a leader sets out to take an organization to a place where, as it turns out, no one else thinks it should be. I'm not saying it's impossible to have success doing that: there have been "maverick" leaders who have been proved (eventually) to be very right, when everyone else thought they were wrong; Steve Jobs of Apple springs to mind. But even if a leader chooses to take the route of most resistance, it's essential that they do it consciously and as a deliberate choice.

I could see that Michael was thinking.

"OK," he said after a short pause. "The board expects me to deliver the desired level of performance. That's just first base. And I have some ideas around that which I hope will surprise and delight the board, but I'm not allowed to talk about that right now."

He glanced at me with a hint of a sly grin.

"Thank you," I said, smiling. "We'll talk about your vision at our next meeting."

"I'm looking forward to that," Michael said, and he clearly meant it. "I have a clear idea of where I'd like to take the organization, but at the moment, I'm still firefighting, like we talked about. What was it you said about a grid? 'Bottom right-hand corner, smoldering but no flames; top left, some flames; top right, ablaze, urgent.'"

I nodded.

"Well, I'm not even sure what's happening anymore. It's clearly not all ablaze, but I'm not even sure what's smoldering and what's actually catching fire. I'm not used to that feeling and I don't like it."

"This process will help," I reassured him. "That's what we're doing here; helping you decide on your priorities and a lot of other fundamentals that will bring everything back under control."

Michael didn't look completely convinced, but I noticed him take a deep breath and relax his shoulders just a little as if maybe these meetings were not a complete waste of his time after all.

"OK," Michael said again, staring into the middle distance. "So. Expectations of the role. One: Deliver the expected organizational performance. Maybe surprise and delight, but I'm not allowed to talk about that." Another sly grin, though not looking directly at me.

"Two: Give direction to the core leadership team, obviously. So that includes the main divisions—Alan and Gabriela. Major internal departments: HR; Legal; R&D; IT; Communications. Then of course Finance—Jimena; Marketing—Kevin; Sales—Jeff. Once we have the new COO in place, a lot of that direction should devolve to him or her, but the board still expects me to be on top of everything.

"Three: Major new drug initiatives. It's just so central to what we do. I need to feel that I am really plugged into progress on that front when Alvin asks me how something is going."

He glanced over at me. "Alvin is our chairman. I must introduce you."

I nodded and smiled to show I knew who Alvin was.

"When he wants to know about something as important as clinical trial results and progress on FDA approval," Michael continued, "I'm not happy saying, 'Oh, I'll have someone update you on that' for something so important. I need to live and breathe that, and I'm sure the board expects me to. I also have some quite radical ideas on that front, but ..."

He glanced at me with another old-fashioned look. I smiled.

"We can talk about that next week, I promise," I said.

"OK," said Michael. "Four: Lead the company within the industry. The CEO is an important figurehead for the company. We're not major players so we need to keep reminding the world that we exist and we're doing great work. Alvin did a brilliant job of that while he was CEO. I think it's fair to say that Alvin 'is' us, if that makes sense. You think of our company, you think of Alvin. I hope I can live up to his example. Our CEO—me—needs to show that we have something to contribute and that we have a voice, and that, in our own small way, we can be industry leaders."

Michael looked combative. I liked what I was seeing.

"And I think finally," said Michael, "Five: Preserve the organizational culture. We've evolved as an organization to the point where we have a very distinctive culture, I believe. It's taken a lot of effort to get to where we are now, and we are very happy with what we have achieved. We want to maintain that culture. Which also means protecting ourselves against a hostile takeover, for example. Which brings us back to the 'deliver the expected performance or better.'"

Michael sat back in his chair.

"I think that's it," he said. "Does that work?"

"That's great," I said. "Thank you."

Something he had said had struck a chord with me.

"We just talked briefly about what the board might expect from the CEO," I said. "Can we talk a bit about what you expect from the board—and I guess from the chairman in particular. From Alvin?"

Michael looked a bit surprised.

"Well, Alvin and I go back quite a long time. We see pretty much eye to eye on things, I think."

"But you will want to do some new things. You may want to do some of the old things differently. How do you think Alvin will react?"

"I'm sure he will be supportive," Michael said, a little shortly.

"I'm sure he will," I agreed. "It's just …"

I hesitated, but Michael looked engaged. He clearly wanted me to finish my train of thought.

"One of the expectations of your role might be that the board wants you to take them with you on this new journey," I suggested. "The board won't expect to lay down rules for you to follow. I'm sure they hope that, as you say, you are going to surprise and delight them. So maybe part of the expectation of your role is that you persuade the chairman and the board that you have the right vision for the company."

Michael gave me another old-fashioned look.

"I know we're not allowed to talk about vision today. My bad!" I said, smiling again. "But you see where I'm going with this? I'm asking you about the expectations of your role. But you're the CEO.

So it works both ways. The board will have certain expectations. But maybe part of the expectation is that you should surprise them, but not literally. That maybe they expect you to persuade Alvin and the board that where you want to take the company is the right place for the company."

Michael looked thoughtful. He didn't make any immediate response.

We had touched on the fact that Michael had yet to appoint a new COO to replace himself in his previous role. He felt—understandably and, to my mind, correctly—that this was a vital appointment and one that he shouldn't rush into. He wanted to settle into his new role before deciding what kind of COO he wanted and exactly what qualities they should bring to the role. I knew that completing his Authentic Leadership Model would help Michael in this process, which was why I was counting my blessings that he had gone along with my insistence that he needed to complete his own leadership model and not just have me work with the rest of the team.

The lack of a new COO was, obviously, a big part of Michael's calendar problem. But it wasn't the only issue.

"This might be a good moment to talk about the COO role?" I suggested. "I would imagine that it's high up on your agenda, because your relationship with the new COO will be key, and clearly that relationship will be a big part of the expectations for your role."

"Well, clearly," said Michael. "It's something we need to resolve as soon as possible, but there are several things I need to reflect on first."

"Absolutely," I said. "As we work on your leadership model, I think a number of things may begin to fall into place."

Michael looked noncommittal.

"Tell me more about the COO role," I ventured.

Michael immediately became animated. We talked at length about the challenges and rewards of the role, how critical it was to the organization, the major challenges he himself had faced in the role, and what he hoped for in his successor.

That conversation filled the rest of our allotted time.

I had arranged to meet with the chief of staff, Alicia, immediately after my meeting with Michael. Alicia's role was not part of the Authentic Leadership Model program, but I was very grateful for her input. If anyone knew the key dynamics of the organization, it was Alicia.

As I stepped into her office, she stood up to greet me. I glanced at her the way someone visiting a sick patient glances at the medical staff, searching for some sign of hope. Almost imperceptibly, she shook her head. After the usual pleasantries and hellos, I asked, brightly but not confidently, "How's the calendar going? And, you know, the whole shotgun thing?"

She smiled in a tight-lipped sort of way but shook her head again. "I shoot 'em down but they keep popping back up. They're like calendar zombies; won't stay dead."

"I'm guessing everything will get better once a new COO is appointed?" I suggested, hesitantly.

"Well, yes," said Alicia. She didn't look entirely convinced. "There's a lot of people who are going to have to lose their dependency on Michael if this is going to work, even when we get a new COO."

I nodded sympathetically and said nothing.

"Like Jeff, for example," said Alicia, without any further prompting.

Jeff was the head of sales who, as far I had gathered, was waging a private war with the head of marketing, Kevin. I was beginning to understand some of the politics of the situation as I started to work with each of the key executives on their leadership models, but the content of those meetings was confidential, obviously, and funnily enough, I tend to compartmentalize in my mind what I am told in such meetings as a result. When I'm talking to Jeff, for example, I suppress the things that I have heard from other people in the organization. If I don't do that, I can't have a direct and honest interaction with Jeff. It was the same now, talking to Alicia.

"Jeff is addicted—I mean *addicted*," said Alicia, "to his relationship with Michael." She looked like an angry mom who felt a schoolmate was demanding too much of her child's time and attention to get help with their own homework. "They're actually very close, and Michael takes a keen interest in sales. I just don't think he notices how much Jeff is leaning on him, and ..." she glanced around a little furtively, although we were the only people in her office. "I feel like he's trying to turn Michael against Kevin in Marketing. There's always a bit of tension between sales and marketing, you know? But Kevin's a bit of a rising star, and I think Jeff feels threatened." She looked me straight in the eye. "But you didn't hear that from me."

I had a feeling that I would sooner break the confidence of a mafia boss than that of Alicia, whose steely-eyed determination was impressive, to say the least. I felt that if Alicia were driving a steam roller flattening asphalt and someone refused to get out of her way, she would decide she could work out how to deal with the mess they were going to make on her asphalt after the job was done.

"Don't get me wrong," said Alicia, softening a little. "Jeff's a great guy. He runs a great sales department. He's a key player for us. It's just that I'm a bit focused on clearing Michael's calendar, and Jeff is part of the problem, not the solution."

"So how's that going?" I asked. "With the calendar."

"Well, like I said, there's a lot of zombie appointments," Alicia told me. "I mean, a key part of the problem is that he's still doing two jobs, right?" She glanced over to make sure I was keeping up.

"He wanted to settle into the role before he appointed his replacement as COO, so right now he's trying to be both COO and CEO, which is not going to work." A hint of dissatisfaction crept back into Alicia's eyes. "But I hope we can get that sorted soon. I'm just not sure that the COO appointment will magically make everything better. Michael is trying to do too much. He will kill himself, he really will. And that's not actually helping the business."

She glanced at me again as if she was afraid she'd said too much.

"Do we know who's in the running for the COO role?" I asked, partly to change the subject.

"I couldn't possibly comment," Alicia fired back, smiling. "But my money is on Kevin or Jimena."

"Tell me about Jimena," I asked.

"Oh, she's great," said Alicia without a beat. "I love her to bits. She's just a bit scary."

I may have flinched slightly. I was trying to imagine a person that Alicia would find scary.

"I mean, scary good!" Alicia jumped in quickly. "She's just on top of everything. She has a kind of 'mind palace,' like Sherlock Holmes. Ask for a number and Jimena can retrieve it. Everyone turns to her when they need to know the bottom line. And she's very generous with her time, you know? She's very approachable. I don't know how she does that and keeps on top of everything else. Now that Michael is so busy, I notice people are turning to Jimena to get a quick heads-up on where things stand and what they should maybe do next."

Alicia looked animated; she was clearly a fan.

"But Kevin is great too," she quickly added. "I mean, it's a tough call. Michael is talking to headhunters about external candidates, but my hunch is that it will be internal. We have a certain culture, and we worry about an outsider coming in and trying to change things just to make their mark. I mean, we really believe in our corporate culture. It's where we think we should be."

I was impressed.

"Can I ask, is Jeff in the running? Or the heads of the two divisions …?" I glanced at my notes. "Alan and Gabriela?"

Alicia looked at me inscrutably. The message was surprisingly clear.

"Tell me about the chairman," I asked. "I haven't met him yet, and if I do it will only be in passing. But what's he like? How do he and Michael get on?"

Alicia was immediately animated again, eyes sparkling, hands moving to reinforce what she was saying.

"Oh, he's wonderful!" she began. "Everyone loves Alvin. He just embodies the company, you know? It feels like he's always been there—which he kinda has—and he sets the tone for everything. We find ourselves thinking, 'How would Alvin deal with this?' when we face any problems. I know Michael does that too. They're very close. Alvin is a bit like …" Alicia paused and then plowed ahead. "He's a bit like Michael's dad, you know? I think I can say that. They're very close, and I know Michael looks up to him. I mean, Alvin's an older generation. I guess that makes him my grandpa. I can relate to that!"

She laughed. It was nice to see her laugh.

"Can I ask one last question?" I said. "What do you think are the key expectations Alvin has of Michael, now that Michael is CEO?"

Alicia's eyes widened a little. "Um, I think that's a little above my paygrade," she said carefully.

I smiled cheerfully and didn't say anything.

"Well," she resumed after a pause, "I guess the CEO needs to set the vision, obviously. And we're not in the major league, but we like to punch above our weight. So I think our CEO needs to be connected with the wider industry—and obviously with the media. Reminding people what a great job we're doing and that it's not just the obvious big names in pharma who are doing good work. And I guess to remind us to keep our game up and that we can achieve great things. That we *have* achieved great things. That's what Alvin was so good at. He made us feel good about what we were doing. Everyone in the business knows Alvin. He's like our figurehead. And he kind of embodies everything we do and what we stand for."

Alicia looked thoughtful. "So, I guess the key expectation is to be a bit more outward facing?" she suggested. "I mean, Michael is a lot like Jimena, in the sense that he seems to know everything, but across the whole company. He's also pretty hot on the financials, by the way; he and Jimena are very tight. But, across the company, he's probably been there and done a lot of it himself, as COO. And if he hasn't done it himself, he's supplied advice and leadership to whoever is or was doing that. There's really not a lot that Michael doesn't know. Which is why everyone turns to him for advice all the time ...."

I thought I could see a few light bulbs starting to glow in Alicia's head, as they were in mine.

"You've been really helpful, Alicia, as ever," I said. "I'd better leave you to get on. Michael had to postpone a couple of appointments with me recently, as you know. It would be really helpful if he and I could keep up the planned weekly meeting cadence, if he can manage that."

"On it!" said Alicia, smiling. "Leave it with me and Janet."

"Are you also happy to keep up a regular catch-up with me yourself?" I asked. "I find it really useful. We could always do a virtual meeting if I'm not in town."

"Sounds good," Alicia said. "Let me know what your calendar looks like."

We looked at each other and laughed.

"Gotta keep on top of those calendars," I agreed.

NICKY DINGEMANS
CHIEF HUMAN CAPITAL OFFICER, OLIVER WYMAN

"I've been thinking a lot recently around the skills and capabilities needed for various roles. We built a competency model probably only five or six years ago that we thought was built to last. But now we are thinking we need to pivot again, because the skills and capabilities required for success in a volatile, uncertain, complex, and ambiguous world are changing more and more rapidly. If we think about what's just happened in the last few months—the advent of generative artificial intelligence (AI) and being able to work with clients in an environment where that's being brought into the mix as well—what does that really mean? The world is changing and evolving faster than ever. I think staying on top of that as an organization and fully understanding what the requirements are and then putting in place scaffolding around an individual when they first take on a new role to help them adapt is essential.

"It's not just about the C-suite. If I think about our environment here at Oliver Wyman, going from consultant to associate, associate to manager, manager to principal—all of these are points where there is a significant shift in role. Consultants are all about being good analysts. Associates are then starting to be real thought leaders and beginning to manage, and then managers are managing whole teams and projects, and then principals are really moving more into the commercial space, and they all have different requirements. So you start to put scaffolding around the individual to help them grow and develop in their new role. And that scaffolding is a lot of developmental type work: coaching, apprenticeship, flying formations, and so on. The same applies to all colleagues including senior leaders. It genuinely is lonely at the top. I think even these most senior roles can benefit from having sponsors and a sounding board and the same kind of scaffolding we put around less senior roles."

MARIA TAYLOR
CHIEF LEARNING OFFICER, UNITED AIRLINES

"I think one of the other challenges is, the more senior you become, the more ambiguous things are and the more agile you need to be. Clarity of expectations and clarity of role become less clear the more senior you are. Because the worst challenge you face when you're more junior is accomplishing a set of tasks or deliverables. When you're more senior and you're in an environment that's always changing, it's reacting to external impacts. It's balancing a number of operational and directional dynamics. If you look at United right now, we're balancing growth, operational excellence, customer service, and then financial pressure. You can do one of those but to try to do all four, you have to make trade-offs. What those trade-offs are create a dynamic tension to be able to do all of those things. And so if you're at the head of an organization or a business unit, you're managing a dynamic of goals and pressures that are competitive."

Summary: Role Expectation

Getting clarity on the expectations of a leadership role is a vital step on the way to being able to develop your Authentic Leadership Model.

Many people turn first to the job description they were given when they were hired or promoted, but that is often an incomplete or even an incorrect description of the role they end up playing.

Understanding the expectations of your role goes beyond the decision rights you have or the straightforward description of what your role involves. It requires thinking in the broadest terms about what you and the organization see as the impact you can make in your role.

At a very senior level, role definition can be very challenging. The COO or CFO role, for example, is theoretically well defined, but the reality is that the definition is often only clear for leaders of a function. Any other responsibility is implicit, which makes C-suite teams often dysfunctional. The CEO role, as Michael is discovering, is even more fluid.

A good example would be Michael's wish for his senior team to become enterprise-wide leaders. It is a common concern of senior leaders that their people are too siloed and function oriented and that they are keen to encourage more enterprise-wide thinking. We all know exactly what this means, but it is a difficult thing to put into a job description in any meaningful sense. This doesn't mean that it is not a real expectation of the role. A common implicit expectation is that the team should work together and support each other to achieve the goals of the organization. This expectation is something that needs to be surfaced and discussed by all parties and should be part of their role descriptions.

A clear understanding of the real expectations of your role is a critical part of the Authentic Leadership Model. I encourage clients to set out their understanding of the expectations of their role and explain, if necessary, why they feel that certain aspects of the job definition should not be ascribed to their role or can remain in the description but are agreed to be a lower priority for them.

The key questions to ask yourself are as follows:

What are the most important things I do?

What are the things that only I can do in the organization?

What are the critical things I must do to enable the team to achieve the vision I have laid out?

Think broadly about what these vital aspects of your role expectations are, including "soft" areas such as relationships, people development, and clearing the way for your team to be successful. All of these things are part of the expectations of your role, even though they may not appear in the role description.

Understanding Your Role Expectations

Your role is defined by:

- The tasks your role needs to undertake and the outcomes it needs to deliver
- The behaviors and attributes that are expected from your role

The original job description and formal decision rights often provide an incomplete or even incorrect description of the role you end up playing.

Discuss the most important expectations of your role with your bosses. Think in broad terms about the impact you can make in the role and the expectations the organization has.

You may want to suggest that some aspects of your job definition should not be ascribed to your role and get agreement that certain things in the current description are low priority for you.

Some useful questions to ask yourself:

- What are the *most important things* I do?
- What are the things *only I can deliver*?
- What are the critical things I must do to *achieve the vision* I have laid out?

Test what you understand the expectations of your role to be against colleagues and your immediate boss.

Do they agree?

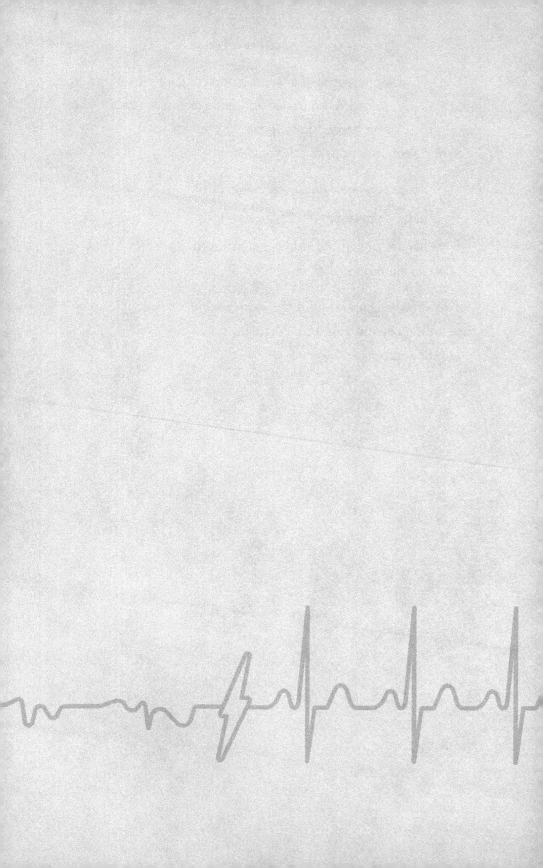

CHAPTER 5

VISION

My next meeting with Michael didn't get postponed. I sensed Alicia's and Janet's hands at work, though I also hoped that Michael might be beginning to see that working through his own Authentic Leadership Model might actually be valuable and might help him resolve some of the issues he was facing.

One of the key problems with leadership shock is that it's hard to step back and see the wood for the trees. There are so many apparently vital issues demanding your attention that it is difficult to understand that these are the symptoms, not the root cause of the situation you suddenly find yourself in.

The root cause is that your previous leadership priorities and your previous approach to leadership are causing you to respond in certain ways to your team and focus on what seem like burning issues when these are no longer the appropriate responses—like, perhaps, doing everything you can to resolve a problem yourself when the burning issues should now be somebody else's problem, not yours.

I felt that Michael and I had come to a very good account of the organization's expectations of his role; it was time to talk about his vision. I sensed that was going to be an easy conversation. I wasn't wrong.

Michael and I settled down in our now accustomed seats, with his coffee and my tea on the glass table between us. Michael still looked distracted and a little haggard. Nothing I had learned from my ongoing conversation with the leadership team about their own Authentic Leadership Models suggested that the situation within the organization had changed much. Everybody seemed to be firefighting; everybody seemed to be desperate for more of Michael's time. There seemed to be a lot of internal conflict. I had heard several more indications that people were turning to Jimena, the CFO, for advice and guidance in Michael's effective "absence." Jimena was well liked and well respected, but there was a worrying sense of drift and absence of leadership. The internecine war between Jeff and Kevin was becoming common knowledge.

I put all these things out of my mind.

"Thanks for finding the time for this meeting, Michael. I know things are very busy."

Michael smiled wanly.

"We talked about the expectations of the CEO's role last week, and I thought we got a lot of clarity. There were a couple of occasions where you wanted to tell me about your vision for the role, and I stopped you because I wanted to focus on role expectation. I'm sorry about that. I promise I won't be such a killjoy today!"

Michael managed a marginally warmer smile.

"So—tell me about your vision for the company. What do you hope to achieve in this role?"

Michael sat forward in his chair. I could sense him collecting his thoughts. Then he relaxed and sat back.

"I thought you'd never ask!" he joked.

For the rest of our hour together, my only contribution was to show that I was listening and engaged and make the occasional encouraging prompt. The words tumbled out of Michael as he outlined plans that, I assume, he had not had the chance to revisit since he last presented them to the board in his final interview for the CEO's role.

"I want us to grow," he told me. "I mean grow quite dramatically. The world is changing. We still develop all of our own new drugs internally. We're very good at it, but it's a long and inevitably painstaking process. There are new biotech companies out there who do nothing else but look for new molecules." He glanced at me. "A 'molecule' is shorthand for a new chemical that might have therapeutic applications," he explained.

I nodded.

"That's all they do. They find new molecules that might be valuable and they sell them to pharma companies like us. They don't have all of the rest of the apparatus and the cost of actually being a pharmaceutical company to worry about; they just look for new molecules. They're doing very well, and some of them are being acquired by pharma companies. I mean, why buy just the molecule if you can buy the whole company?" He smiled. "It's not necessarily cheaper than the old in-house route, but it's definitely faster."

"And then there are other biotech companies who are doing clever things with AI, like discovering that a drug that has been licensed for treating one condition might actually be very effective in treating another, completely different condition. And that can also mean that a drug we have developed that has now become generic because its patent has expired suddenly has a whole new lease of life for treating a different condition. We should be exploring that avenue."

Michael was still in full flow. I smiled encouragingly.

"I think perhaps we could also acquire some other traditional, small pharma companies. I mean, I think we should go all out for organic growth, but that takes time. I think we could really kick start the process by acquiring some companies that maybe take us in a new direction. I'm thinking we could make some acquisitions that would effectively create a whole new division of the company. Maybe two. That would be a radical new departure for us. I'm still talking to Alvin and the board about it."

I was used to seeing Michael looking stressed and a little tired. The years fell off him as the ideas poured out. We clearly didn't have to worry about "the vision thing." Michael had the vision. What we needed to do was get him out of the leadership shock he was experiencing and fully functional in his new role.

"What about your vision internally?" I prompted. "You've just talked about new divisions. But do you have any ideas about how the existing structure would work differently? About how people's roles might be different?"

It was obviously the right question to ask. Michael was off again, like a sprinter off the blocks.

"It's not necessarily the structure," he said. "We talked about the COO's role. My old role."

He glanced at me, and I nodded.

"And I think maybe that role could be structured a little differently. You'll have to leave that with me; I'm still working on it."

I nodded again.

"But I think the main thing is …" Michael looked briefly out the window at the morning sky. It was a beautiful spring day. I think we both wished, briefly, that we were talking outside and not in the office.

"I would like the team to think bigger," Michael said finally. "I'd like them to think of themselves as being leaders enterprise-wide, if you know what I mean. I want everyone to be thinking about how we grow and achieve the new vision and about whether it's the right vision or maybe they have some other idea. And I'd like to give them more exposure to the board of directors. I want the board to get to know them and hear what they're trying to achieve. I don't want mine to be the only face the board gets to see."

"Would that be a new departure?" I asked.

"Well, that was pretty much Alvin's way," said Michael. "You probably gather that Alvin is …" He hesitated. "I think 'revered' is probably the right word. He's revered by everyone. He's been the face of the company for a long time, internally and externally. Alvin dealt with the board and the chairman, and everyone was happy with that, but I'd like to loosen things up a bit. I'd like the board to get to know more of the wider leadership team."

"We're too siloed," Michael continued. "I don't want Kevin to think he's just 'the marketing leader,' for example. I want him to think he's an enterprise-wide leader with special expertise in marketing. Does that make sense?"

"That makes sense," I said.

"And Jimena shouldn't just be leading finance," he went on. "She should be offering leadership across the whole enterprise. Jimena is actually a good role model, because she already does that to a large extent. People already turn to her for guidance on a range of issues. She's in a very strong position to replace me as COO, as you're probably aware."

He glanced at me, and I did my best to look inscrutable, but I had a bad feeling I was doing as badly as Alicia when I'd asked her whether the two divisional heads were in the frame for the COO's role.

"I still have a completely open mind regarding that appointment," Michael said quickly, as if he was reading my mind. "I'm interviewing in the next few weeks. I need someone who sees things the way I do. What I'm hoping to achieve is going to make huge demands on the leadership team, and I need a COO who's on the same page as me. It's not just a question of running a tight ship. I need someone who can help me do things differently."

Michael trailed off again, but his eyes were still bright, and he looked happy.

"Sounds great," I said, and I meant it. Everything suddenly seemed a lot more optimistic.

"Do you know …" I started, and then paused. Michael was staring out the window again, and I didn't want to break his train of thought.

He looked back at me. "No, go ahead," he said, encouragingly.

"You remember that we agreed that your purpose was 'Working as a team to make a difference in people's lives'?"

Michael nodded.

"Well, the team are also people whose lives you could make a difference to," I suggested. "The great thing about fulfilling our purpose is that it gives us energy. It energizes us. We can't spend all our time focused on our purpose, because life isn't like that. But when we do, it fills our tank. It's how we most want to spend our time and it fills our emotional tank. I suspect that helping your team to grow and develop would actually fit your purpose and help energize you. I think you would get a lot back from doing that."

I meant it. Michael looked a bit bashful.

"I mean ..." he started. "It's a great team. They don't need me to set them free or wave a magic wand in their lives. But I feel ..."

He'd gone again, briefly. I waited.

"This is going to sound like I'm blowing my own trumpet," he began. I made dismissive gestures, waving the idea away.

"When I was COO, I was the guy with all the answers," he said. I smiled.

Michael went on to tell me that he felt his relationship with his team was defined primarily by people coming to him for advice on how to solve some issue, which he would do his best to supply. He told me he felt he should stop doing that—that he should encourage the team to offer their own solutions, even when he felt he had the answer. He also said he felt sure he would not have all of the answers once the company began to move in the new direction he had planned for it because this was a new, uncertain future and a new world. He wanted to feel that his team were coming up with their own solutions and their own ideas.

And then Michael said something else I'd been hoping to hear.

"I need to be less involved in the day-to-day," he said. "I tend to roll my sleeves up and get stuck in to help fix issues and get things done. And I'm still doing that as well as all the new things I want to get done, and now I don't seem to have time to eat or sleep, let alone to think."

"That's what we're going to fix," I said seriously.

Michael smiled a thin, tight smile.

"If we can fix that even this much ..." He held up his thumb and forefinger with maybe an inch of space between them. "It will have been worth it!"

"We can do better than that," I said.

On the flight back to Denver, I was thoughtful. I had begun working on the Authentic Leadership Models for the rest of the team, so I was beginning to get more of a feel for the leadership team organization as a whole.

I was impressed. The fact that the heads of division, Alan and Gabriela, did not seem to be seriously in the running for the COO role had made me wonder unfairly about their abilities. In fact, they were both highly able leaders, running what in effect was a small pharma company each. But I could see how the inevitable specialty of their roles would make it difficult—not impossible, but difficult—for either of them to make the necessary leap to taking on the running of the company. Both were also more science than business oriented. Again, not an overwhelming obstacle in a pharma company, but I could see that they might not be the ideal candidate for Michael's key support role as he set out to make quite radical changes to the organization.

Jimena, the head of finance, was as impressive as she sounded, completely on top of her brief and with a shrewd grasp of the key issues facing every part of the organization. I know it's not all about the numbers, but knowing everything about all the numbers isn't a bad way to understand what makes an organization tick.

Kevin, the head of marketing, was equally impressive, with a clear grasp of the company's position in the pharma market and, I felt, of the general direction of the market. He seemed a very incisive thinker. When he talked to me about where the company and the pharma industry were likely headed, I learned new things.

Jeff, the head of sales, came as something of a surprise. Alicia's protective instincts had probably given her a negative view of Jeff.

Or perhaps I should say that her protective instincts had given her a perspective on Jeff that caused me to get a negative view of him.

From her point of view, Jeff was demanding too much of Michael's time, so he was part of the problem, but I was beginning to understand where Jeff was coming from. Jeff was very much the salesman: charming and engaging, with great communication skills, but also very driven. Jeff liked to win. He wanted to close the sale. He also clearly very much wanted the COO role. He sensed that he had stiff competition from Jimena and Kevin, so he was doing everything he could to get himself at the forefront of Michael's mind. He was "doing a job" on Michael and doing all he could to undermine Kevin. I couldn't blame him for that.

As for Michael, the more time I spent with him, the more impressed I became. He was clearly suffering from leadership shock, and we had a lot more work to do on his Authentic Leadership Model before I would know exactly what would allow him to set his priorities and decide exactly how he wanted to lead the organization, but the root of the problem was already clear.

Michael, like almost every leader before him in the same situation, was finding that the personal strengths and the leadership approach that had served him so well in the past were not what would allow him to succeed in his new role. His relationship with the leadership team was still dictated by the things that had made him such a successful COO: the guy who knows everything; the man with all the answers; a Mr. Fixit for the whole organization. His approach needed to change, radically and quickly.

I didn't know exactly what would trigger Michael into seeing the way forward, but I knew from experience that working our way through Michael's Authentic Leadership Model would lead, at some point, to a revelation—the all-important "ah-ha!" moment when everything suddenly falls into place and the picture becomes clear. You never know exactly at what point in the Authentic Leadership Model that moment will come, but it always does. It's a very satisfying moment for me. It is, in fact, what energizes me and fills my own emotional tank.

I was looking forward to our next session. I was hoping Michael was too, and I was beginning to feel that our sessions were no longer an unavoidable chore for him: a kind of penance I had demanded as the price of me undertaking to work on the Authentic Leadership Models of the rest of the team. I sensed that he was beginning to get a glimpse of the potential value of our discussions.

MARIA TAYLOR
CHIEF LEARNING OFFICER, UNITED AIRLINES

"You can have a multiyear vision. In fact, you should have a North Star and a multiyear vision, you just need to recognize that the initiatives and the tactics that get you there will have to be dynamic and change. In my role as chief learning officer at United, I came in in 2019 with the same vision, which was to have best-in-class training for the organization, enabled by technology, responsive to the business, and with great outcomes and financial discipline. The tactics that I've used to get there have had to change for each group in each circumstance. And so the ability to learn and be agile is one of the most important leadership tenets today, I think, and then the ability to bring your people along and adapt the resource base. I don't know that we were taught that in business school."

Summary: Vision

A leader's vision is a key element of the Authentic Leadership Model. It provides direction on where you want to spend your time and on how you want to spend it.

Your vision can be developed at different levels: what you want to accomplish as an individual, what you want the team to achieve, and where you want the organization to be in a few years' time. The broader the vision the harder it is to fulfill, but senior leaders will have a broader scope. Fundamentally, your vision should be at the level the organization expects around the outcomes you should achieve.

Your vision is simply the description of a future state, often in a relatively near time frame such as two to three years from now. It is important to go through the thought process of making choices about where you want to focus your time and energy.

Visions can be presented as taglines or bullet points or in the form of a few sentences. The critical factor is going through the process of deciding where to concentrate your time and energy, rather than how the vision is articulated. Vision is all about choice. Like any good strategy, it should tell you what you do less of; it should tell you what you most want to achieve, but it should not tell you how you are going to achieve it.

Vision can be broad or specific. The more specific the vision, the easier it is for the leader to make choices about where they want to spend their time. When I ask my clients to develop their vision, I suggest they think about three different stakeholders: a member of the team, the organization as a whole, and an outside stakeholder— perhaps a customer or an industry organization—and then identify what the client wants these stakeholders to say about them. Thinking about those three different perspectives and what they want those different stakeholders to say they have achieved in the two- or three-year time frame helps to make their vision more specific.

Remember to think back to the expectations of your role. It is possible to have a vision that introduces some entirely new and unexpected goals but it is important to make sure everyone understands this part of your vision and agrees that it would be desirable and represents a good use of your and your team's time.

Setting Your Vision

Your vision is a description of the future at a certain point in time. People may feel that a vision needs to be complex but that is not true. It can be as simple as, "What do you want to achieve in the next two years and what does that look like?"

A way to get to the vision is to ask yourself what you want the following stakeholders to say you have achieved in those two years:

- A team member
- The organization as a whole
- A client, customer, or industry organization

What is the *minimum* you would want them to recognize you have achieved?

What would confirm you had achieved *everything* in your vision?

Your vision should help you make choices about where you spend your time and energy.

- What do you need to do *more of* to achieve your vision?
- What do you need to do *less of*?
- Is your vision *bold* enough?
- Is it *too ambitious*?

EXERCISE:

Think back to the expectations of your role. *Will your vision deliver what is expected of you?*

Your vision can include things that are not in the original expectations of your role.

- Does the organization agree that these aspects of your vision are *desirable* and represent a good use of your time?
- Will achieving your vision be seen as *success*?

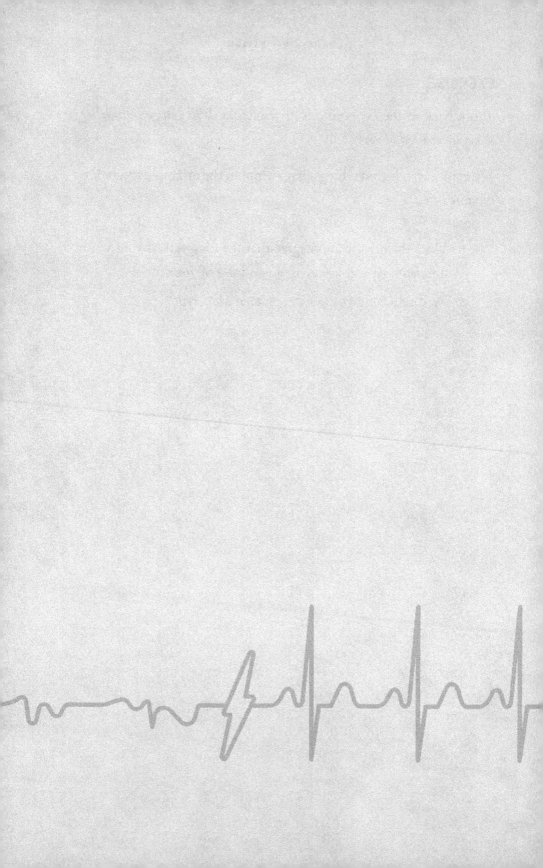

CHAPTER 6

PRIORITIES

After a few days back at the office, I caught up with Alicia via a Zoom call. It was April, and it was a beautiful spring day in Colorado. That's always nice, but it doesn't really mean a lot. You can get six inches of snow in Colorado the next day, even in April.

Alicia's face came up on the screen. Alicia is always feisty, always full of energy, but I have to say even she was looking a little drawn.

"Alicia, hi! How's it going?" I asked a little tentatively.

"Hi, Pete. Well … it's not great."

"How's the …" I was going to ask about Michael's calendar, of course, but Alicia was ahead of me.

"Don't ask. We've got interviews for the COO role over the next few weeks," she said, "which is kinda great, obviously, but it's not helping the calendar. I've been shooting up anything nonessential, like we agreed." She smiled, briefly. "But I've still got this crazy backlog. There's people Michael really wants to talk to about new stuff. Like, the future and everything, you know? And I just can't fit them in. It's all about firefighting."

"Can you tell me what the main stuff filling up his calendar is?" I asked. "The bread-and-butter stuff?"

"Oh yeah, I can tell you," said Alicia. She sounded a little sarcastic, as if I'd asked her what she actually did all day.

"First, we have all the weeklies. Michael doesn't want to leave people unsupported until we appoint the new COO, so he's keeping up his weekly meetings with everyone. You know: Jeff, Kevin, Jimena, Gabriela, Alan. And HR, and R&D, and Legal. And IT. And PR ... Oh, and me, though I've been shooting my own appointments up a lot lately. If I can catch Michael for a few minutes here and there, we can manage.

"Then he has his new weekly meeting with Alvin, which I guess is important.

"Then there's all the external meetings that Michael used to run as COO, or at least sit in on—meetings with major customers and vendors. And then there's the internal stuff that tends to end up on the COO's desk even if someone else is running it—you know, crazy stuff: security; catering; some big HR issue; a new press release; the new R&D lab; creating new green spaces on campus!" Alicia's voice was rising slightly. She laughed, a little harshly.

"Then there's the open-door policy of course. That's my favorite. If you have a problem, you can just walk right into Michael's office if he's like, chilling out, not doing much, you know?" Her voice crept up another quarter tone. "That's the way Michael has always wanted it."

"How are you doing yourself, Alicia?" I asked, carefully.

She drew in a deep breath.

"Thank you for asking," she said. She looked like she meant it.

"It's OK, it really is," she said finally. "And I'm OK. But it can't go on. Michael is doing too much. The COO appointment will make a big difference, obviously. But I feel like more has to change than just finding a new COO, you know? I feel like something fundamental has to change or Michael will just blow up. I might even blow up, and …" she paused.

You can't really glance at someone in a Zoom meeting, but Alicia's eyes flashed toward the camera of her desktop, and it felt like she was glancing at me. Her voice switched to a conspiratorial whisper.

"And the whole company might just blow up."

She looked at me earnestly.

"Everything was just perfect before, you know? Alvin was just the perfect CEO. Michael was the safest pair of hands as COO. It was just like clockwork; a well-oiled machine. And suddenly, nothing works any more. Nobody seems to know what they're doing. It's all going *al infierno. Al infierno sobre ruedas.*"

She looked at me.

"Do the English say that? To hell on wheels?"

Alicia found the fact that I grew up in England and the remnants of my English accent endlessly amusing.

"We would probably say 'to hell in a handcart,'" I said. "I have no idea why we say that. I don't know why it would be a handcart."

"There's no explaining the crazy English," Alicia said, laughing.

I took it on the chin and got back to business.

"I know the calendar is still full," I said.

Alicia rolled her eyes and pulled a face.

"But can we keep my next few meetings with Michael in place? We are actually making good progress. A few more meetings should begin to make a real difference."

"If you can help Michael, you can get as much access as I can manage," said Alicia, earnestly.

"Can you also do me a massive favor?" I asked. "Can you make some kind of record about what you told me earlier? You know—how Michael actually spends his time? The regular meetings with key people, the meetings about things like green spaces on campus. How much time the 'open-door' policy actually takes up?"

Alicia stared off-camera for a spell and absent-mindedly scratched the side of her head with a perfectly manicured nail.

"Leave it with me," she said after a while. "I'll need to talk to Janet as well."

"Sounds great," I said. "I'm really grateful."

Alicia smiled, and we both hit the "end meeting" button to finish our call.

Alicia managed to help Janet keep my meetings with Michael.

The next time we met, Michael looked genuinely exhausted—not just stressed and a bit haggard but really running on empty. I tried to chat about a recent international rugby game, because I knew that was a shared interest, but he was distracted. The only thing Michael cared about right now was work, so I decided we might as well dive straight in.

"We talked about the expectation of your role a few weeks back," I began.

Michael started to look a little more focused.

"And I felt you were comfortable with what we settled on," I continued.

I glanced at my notes.

"Deliver the expected organizational performance," I read. "Ideally, surprise and delight!"

Michael managed a faint smile.

"Give direction to the leadership team; stay focused working on major drug initiatives …"

Michael took over without having to look at my list. "Lead for the company within the industry and preserve the organizational culture," he said. "I remember."

I smiled.

"Does that still work for you?" I asked.

"I've been thinking about that," Michael said, thoughtfully. "I think there's one more, which is probably obvious. So obvious that I didn't think of it at first. But I think 'Lead the organization as a whole' should be on the list if the organization is going to change and grow the way I want it to."

He looked at me.

"Am I allowed to talk about vision today?"

"Sure!" I said, grinning. "Any time. The embargo is lifted."

"If the company is going to go through these changes successfully," Michael went on, "I need to be bringing everyone with me. And I mean everyone. I don't want to give direction to the leadership team and then say, 'That's it, guys. Off you go and do that. You lead the organization while I focus on other things—on growth, or on dealing with the industry as a whole, or whatever it might be.' Because I don't think it would work. I don't think it would be fair of me to put that on their shoulders, and I don't think it would really work. I think there has to be one voice."

He looked over at me.

"Has anyone told you about how we say, 'What would Alvin do?'"

"Alicia told me," I said. "And also, I guess a few of your colleagues as we've been working on their Authentic Leadership Models. So, um … yeah. I have heard that!"

"Uh huh," said Michael, smiling. "It's a bit of a thing with us. And I found myself thinking not, 'What would Alvin do?' but 'What *did* Alvin do when he was CEO?' And what he did was supply leadership to everyone. Literally everyone throughout the company. We all knew what we wanted to do and what we thought was the right thing to do because of Alvin and what he taught us. So I need to take on that role. *Obviously*, like I said. It was just so obvious, I managed to miss it."

"That happens," I agreed. "One of the most important things about the leadership model," I said, "is that it's a living document. Things change."

I looked directly at Michael, because I wanted to make sure he understood what I was trying to say.

"The expectations of your role might change over time. Or you might choose to put a different emphasis on certain aspects of the expectations of your role over time," I went on. "And your priorities might change as a result—we're going to talk about your priorities in a moment. But the leadership model is primarily about metacognition. It's about coming to understand why we are doing what we do: what we want to achieve and why we lead the way we do. Once we understand that, we can always check back and see whether what we are actually doing fits with our purpose, and what's expected of our role, and what we want to achieve, and how we want to offer leadership. Does that make sense?"

Michael nodded and looked thoughtful. I thought I might have detected a glimmer of hope, but maybe that was wishful thinking.

I had a new idea.

"Talking about vision," I began. "I tend to think of vision in terms of three-year cycles. I mean, you might have a vision that will take the organization ten years to accomplish, but that's a longer time frame than most people like to think about, right?"

Michael seemed to agree.

"So, imagine you've been CEO for three years. What do you want the board to say about what you've achieved? What do you want the executive team to say? And finally, what do you want employees to say about your tenure?" I looked at him again. "So, three years, three groups of people giving their assessment. What do you think?"

Michael stayed quiet for some time.

"OK," he said finally. "I think, for the board, I want them to say that I delivered what I promised—but I also want them to say the company has changed. I want them to know we've grown by X percent or whatever we agree on, but also that we're in a better place as an organization than we were when I took on the role. I mean, a better place in terms of being equipped to deal with a changing future. I'm not suggesting we're in a bad place now," he added quickly.

I nodded reassuringly.

"OK. Executive team. What I really want—and I mean this—is for them to say that I've helped them do what they most want to do. I want them to feel empowered."

"I mean, I'd also like them to do what I ask them to do, obviously," Michael said, looking at me over the top of his glasses with a slight smile. "But I genuinely want them to feel like they've been allowed to do what they most want to do to get to where we need to be. I don't want to drag people along or put a gun to their heads. But I also feel that we have the right team and we all want the same thing. I don't have any serious reservations about anyone. We wouldn't be able to work together as a team as well as we do if that wasn't the case. But I would like them to say that I helped them do what they wanted to do, not that they did what I asked them to do just to make me happy."

I nodded again.

"And then the company as a whole," said Michael. "That's tricky. I guess I'd be happy if we were doing well, and it was obvious we were doing well, and people could see that the things I'd set out to do had worked for the company. So, I guess the bottom line for that is people feeling proud about what they do and confident that the company has a good future. That our employees know they can thrive with us and have a good future for themselves."

Michael sat back a little in his chair.

"That's great, thanks," I said. "So we've identified what we think are the expectations of the role, and you've told me about your vision—the things you want to achieve over maybe a three-year time frame. These two things drive what should be your main priorities. And you've told me you want the board to feel that you've delivered on what you promised and also put the company in a place where it's equipped to handle whatever the future might bring."

Michael nodded.

"And you want your colleagues to feel empowered to achieve the things they personally want to achieve, and you want the company as a whole to feel that the company is successful, and everyone is part of that and can share in that."

I glanced at Michael to check I was summarizing correctly.

"That's about it," he acknowledged, smiling slightly.

"So, what are your priorities?" I asked. "What would you select as the things you really want to achieve and the things you feel you *must* achieve to see yourself as having succeeded in the role?"

Michael didn't immediately respond.

"I think maybe one way to approach this," I suggested, "is that a) we want all those things to happen, right? You want to fulfill all those expectations and you want to achieve all the things on your wish list for your vision. But also, b) you don't have to achieve all of them yourself. In fact, there's almost none of those things you can achieve by yourself. Maybe your relationship with the board and with your team. But even then, you can only control your side of that relationship. You can never be sure how people will respond."

I was concerned I was maybe getting a bit philosophical, but I plowed ahead.

"So we want all those things to happen but you can't do any of them all by yourself. So what does that say about your personal priorities? What are the things that are burningly urgent to you? And also—which is kind of the flipside—what are you *not* going to do? What are the things where you think, 'That needs to happen, but it's not going to be me that does that?'"

Michael was staring out the window, deep in thought.

"One final thought," I said. "Just a tool that some people find useful. If we're considering what you should and shouldn't be doing, a useful way of thinking about that might be what we talked about earlier. Not, 'What should I be doing?' but 'What should the CEO be doing?' What do you think is essential to the role, as opposed to what your personal inclinations might be?"

"These are big questions," I said, finishing up. "This is at the heart of the choices you make going forward. What do you think?"

Michael was silent for quite a long time. I was happy with the fact that he didn't mind that we could sit there for a while without having to say anything.

"OK," he said finally and decisively. One of the things I was increasingly getting to like about Michael was his thoughtfulness and decisiveness.

"I'm going to deliver the numbers," he said, in a tone of voice that brooked no argument. "That's going to happen. I don't make promises on bottom line stuff and not deliver."

I nodded in an affirmative, "Damn right!" sort of way.

"And then I'm going to surprise and delight." He looked at me slightly impishly. "Which I'm now allowed to talk about, right?"

"Surprise and delight!" I acknowledged, smiling. "So what do you think that means for your priorities in the role?"

"OK," Michael said again. "This is not an easy question."

Michael and I talked about priorities for the rest of our allocated time. It was immediately clear that growth was at the top of Michael's agenda. He was determined to make the company bigger and stronger. He told me he was open to a conversation with his colleagues about whether it could grow organically or by acquisition, but it seemed clear to me that he had his eye set on at least some level of acquisitions. That he was in a hurry and that organic growth wasn't going to be able to deliver what he had in mind fast enough.

Something else that emerged very clearly was Michael's interest in developing new drugs and encouraging a culture of quite radical innovation. It was obvious that acquiring new companies and making new partnerships wasn't just about getting bigger as a company, it was about building a creative, agile organization at the cutting edge of drug development.

"We don't have the same R&D budget as the big guys, obviously," Michael said. "But, funnily enough, a lot of the big guys are buying in specialist new companies that are working on interesting new molecules. They're finding that process cheaper and faster than the old model of doing everything themselves, in-house. And they don't have a monopoly on that. They've got deeper pockets than we have, but maybe we can be faster and smarter. And maybe some of these companies would rather partner with us than with them."

As Michael was telling me this, I could see the stress falling away from him again. He was animated and engaged. He looked like a war horse champing at the bit, eager to start the charge.

As our conversation went on, it became clear that he was entirely genuine about empowering the senior leadership team and that he wanted to encourage real independence of thought. He talked about how he wanted people to surprise him by driving through initiatives he hadn't thought of himself and that he wanted to "let a hundred flowers bloom." But I still wasn't quite sure how he saw his relationship with the senior team developing. Even though we'd had the earlier conversation about his needing to back off from his current hands-on relationship with the team, it was obvious he wasn't sure how that was going to work. I felt it wasn't that he didn't trust his colleagues not to cope on their own—far from it—but that he felt obligated to keep offering them his support; that he would feel guilty if he didn't still make himself available to them.

We also talked about his relationship with Alvin and with the rest of the board. For the first time, I thought I detected the slightest hint of irritation from Michael about this relationship with Alvin.

"Don't get me wrong," he started. "Alvin and I are more than colleagues, we're good friends. He's been my boss and mentor for however many years it is now, and we've been through a lot together. There were some difficult years for the company a few years back. Before your time," he said, with a smile, looking over at me. "I admire the guy immensely, and he's been a big influence on me."

He paused.

"But …?" I suggested.

Michael started a little and looked almost guilty.

"Well …" he began and hesitated again. I could sense a little internal debate going on in his head, then he clearly came to a decision.

"OK," he said suddenly. "I can't say I've thought this through very well. But I think it might be important. I feel like our relationship needs a bit of a reset." He looked at me a little challengingly, as if I might be horrified by what I was hearing. I was not horrified, I was delighted.

"It's just that at the moment, our relationship is the same as it's always been," Michael continued. "We have our weekly meetings and Alvin is being his usual supportive self, but I'm not finding them as valuable as I used to."

Michael looked for a moment as if he could hardly believe his own words. I nodded encouragingly.

"He's offering support and advice as ever, like I said, but I don't know for sure what I want him to support me in doing, do you know what I mean?"

He looked at me with a sense of real inquiry. I nodded again.

"What I actually need is to decide what I want to do with the company. I mean, I know exactly what I want to do in the broad sense, it's what you and I are talking about here." He looked at me again, and I felt for the first time that Michael was confiding in me as opposed to dutifully answering the questions I put to him. "I want to flesh out those ideas and brainstorm some of the crazier stuff, and I'm not sure Alvin is the right person for that."

He looked as if he felt he had said something sacrilegious, but he carried on.

"I'm not sure Alvin will instinctively support some of the things I'd like to do. He's very wedded to the idea that we do it all ourselves;

that we keep everything in-house and develop our own new drugs and build the company from within, and I think that might be too slow. I think we're going to acquire stuff from outside and buy in some talent and some innovative ideas. It's not that I think we can't do it ..." He looked at me again as if he felt he was committing an act of betrayal. "It's just that it will take too long. We need to get bigger fast."

He sat back, looking a little shocked and exhausted.

"Can I suggest ...?" I started.

It was Michael's turn to nod and look encouraging.

"We talked about how one of the expectations of your role is you taking the board with you; you persuading the board that the direction you want to take the company in is the right one. I mean, obviously, right? If you don't take the board with you, that's a problem."

Michael nodded again.

"And the easiest way to the board is through the chairman, Alvin. And you have a great relationship with Alvin, but it's changing. It needs to change. Because Alvin's not running the company anymore, you are. Part of his job before was to make sure you had the resources and support from the organization to get things done and achieve the company's goals. But he was the man setting those goals. Now it's you. So Alvin's role is still to support you, but not in the same way. You're in control of the strategy. You've got all the resources at your disposal. What you need from Alvin is for him to sell your vision to the board. He needs to understand exactly what you want to achieve, and he needs to be able to talk convincingly to the board about why what you want to do is the best possible thing for the organization. You need to take Alvin with you. You need to manage Alvin, in a way. I mean, in the nicest possible way!" I added hastily.

Michael looked thoughtful.

We talked on, and time flew by.

"I hope you found that as useful as I did," I said when our time was up. Michael smiled. He looked happier than I had seen him since the moment we met.

"We haven't had time to make any decisions about your priorities today," I said as I collected my few things together, "but that's fine. We need to circle back and make decisions about your priorities after we've worked through the rest of your leadership model. It's not a linear process; everything feeds into everything else and changes everything."

"Next week," I said, winding up, "I'd like to talk about the strengths you feel you bring to the new role. The things you feel you can leverage most to achieve what you want."

"Sounds good!" said Michael, still smiling.

"How are the COO interviews going?" I asked as I was heading for the door.

Michael looked suddenly thoughtful again.

"They're going very well," he said. "They are all hugely impressive candidates. We're lucky to have so much talent to choose from. But it's going to be a tough call. Very tough."

I smiled and left Michael's office, saying my goodbyes to Janet as I walked through the outer room and headed for the lift.

COREY MUÑOZ
FORMER CHIEF TALENT OFFICER, KPMG LLP

"Most people moving to a more senior role focus on the transition: the leveling up, the new responsibilities, the new scope, all those sorts of things. But there's another very important piece we often forget, which is, what do you *stop* doing? I think that's what people can miss. A lot of times when leaders transition, they're keeping some of the same approaches, styles, activities, those sorts of things, while trying to level up. You can get consumed by the new scope, the new responsibilities of the role, but you actually have to stop doing a set of things too, or you will never level up to the degree that you need to."

MARIA TAYLOR
CHIEF LEARNING OFFICER, UNITED AIRLINES

"Everything we do should be aligned with our vision, regardless of the initiative. Keeping that front of mind is really important, and how it aligns to the overall enterprise goals. And then in terms of priority, looking at what's the biggest impact. What's the biggest objective and impact that you can have against those versus smaller things? Biggest impact, biggest gap. I personally tend to spend my time in the envision and design stages. And then once we get into execution, or build and execute, I can allow the team to take over. Sometimes there are crises as well and you have to respond to the crises. I believe in fanning out and diving deep. Understanding that dynamic is important and reacting to that dynamic can be uncomfortable. It's also really important to give yourself space to step back and think more strategically, and to find ways to help your team to do that. I'm a big fan of the innovation process and design thinking and some of those things. It's really important as a leader."

Summary: Priorities

The Authentic Leadership Model is a tool that helps you make choices and prioritize the things you choose to spend your time on. Thinking about your purpose, your role expectations, and your vision helps you to be certain that these are authentic priorities, grounded in the things you know you want to achieve.

Being clear about your priorities is impactful—because it is going to help you deliver your vision—and important, because it helps you fulfill the role in the way the organization expects.

Deciding on your priorities is an iterative process within the Authentic Leadership Model. You might initially choose a priority but then realize it is not part of your purpose, your role expectations, or your vision. You might feel, for example, that it should be a priority of yours to develop the capabilities of your team, but when you go back and look at your vision and your purpose, or you look at your role expectations, you may realize that developing the capability of your team should be part of somebody else's priority. This might lead you to question whether you have the right role expectations and whether your purpose is genuinely what you most want to do. If a priority feels uncomfortable with your stated purpose, it is possible that you have not stated your purpose correctly and need to rethink it, but it is more likely that the priority you are considering is not a true priority.

Having fewer, more impactful priorities is better than having more, less impactful priorities. If you find you have a long list of priorities, there is something wrong in your definition of your purpose and vision: they have failed to help you decide what is critically important. Having too many priorities can take us back into leadership shock.

The key thing to focus on is *change* and the priorities that are going to affect where you spend your time. When I work with clients, we usually come up with three to five priorities that will change where they spend their time and energy. Before we get to that point, we will typically have explored perhaps ten different priorities and tested those against purpose, vision, and role expectations to make sure they truly are the most impactful priorities. It is important to capture this list of potential priorities and write them down, because we will continue to come back to them as we work our way through the Authentic Leadership Model.

CHOOSING YOUR PRIORITIES

Your purpose, your vision, and the expectation of your role help shape your priorities.

When your priorities reflect these three things, you can be certain they are grounded in what you want to achieve.

Purpose + Vision + Role = Priorities

When your priorities fit your purpose, you will feel fulfilled and energized in pursuing them.

EXERCISE:

Think of around *ten* possible priorities for your role.

Test those against your purpose, vision, and role expectations.

Whittle them down to between *three* and *five* priorities.

Write them down.

If you make these things your priorities, *will they deliver* your vision and role expectations and follow your purpose?

Is something *missing*?

Is something *not a key priority* after all?

As you work through the Authentic Leadership Model, and as time goes by, *revisit* your priorities to confirm they are the things most likely to achieve your vision and fulfill your role expectations.

CHAPTER 7

THE VALUE I BRING

I had been having my regular conversations with Michael's senior team as we worked on their individual Authentic Leadership Models, and I was learning a lot more about them as individuals and about their dynamics as a team. I have to say, I was liking what I found. Michael wasn't wrong to say that the team had great individual strengths and, more importantly, that there was a genuine sense of being a team. There were the usual small niggles and grievances, but in general everyone appreciated their colleagues' strengths and contribution and there was a palpable sense that they knew where the company was going and what they could do to help get it there.

But …

There was a growing sense of the past tense in a lot of what they had to say to me. A sense of loss of direction and not knowing what to do to keep things moving forward. I noticed a lot of references to "What would Alvin do?" and a sense of something like nostalgia for the old days of certainty. Michael was clearly much admired by his colleagues, and I sensed a real affection for him also, but there was a feeling of drift. A momentous change had occurred—Alvin had moved up to chairman and Michael had taken over as CEO—and the dust had not yet settled. When I asked about future plans, everyone seemed suddenly uncertain. What did that future look like? What would their role be in this new future? No one had a clear answer. In exactly the same way that Michael seemed overwhelmed and not fully in control of events, the team seemed rudderless, unsure of what was needed from them or what they should be focused on.

As I worked on the team's individual leadership models, it was Alan and Gabriela, the two heads of division, who seemed most relaxed and focused. If they were missing their previous relationship with Michael, it clearly wasn't having a big impact on their day-to-day roles. They had both thrown their hats into the ring for the new COO role, and they were both strong contenders, but I got the sense that they were a little insulated from the changes affecting the rest of the organization. They were running their own divisions, had a clear view of what those divisions needed to deliver, and were happily working away, as they always had, to deliver the goods. As we worked on their Authentic Leadership Models, they were both able to give me a very clear view of what they felt were the key expectations of their role, what was their vision for what they wanted to achieve, and the priorities they had set to achieve that vision. But I didn't get a sense of any broader vision for the company as a whole. Maybe I was being unfair.

I found that I was warming to Jeff, the head of sales. I had thought that Jeff was simply trying to make sure that he had Michael's full attention at a time when everyone was jockeying for position in the bid for the COO's role. And I had definitely been influenced by Alicia's view of Jeff as being one of the chief demanders of Michael's time; Alicia was very persuasive. But I had come to see also that there was a genuine relationship between Jeff and Michael. Jeff looked up to Michael and relied on him for advice and support, but he was also fiercely loyal and supportive of Michael in his turn. It was hard not to like Jeff, which I guess is the sign of a great salesperson. There was a real rivalry between him and the other contenders for the COO role, but it was friendly. Jeff didn't run down his colleagues or undermine them. I was impressed by the general atmosphere of "team spirit."

Kevin, the head of marketing, was harder to read. He was open, likable, intelligent, just slightly academic—he had a doctorate in Biophysical Chemistry and talked excitedly about the science behind the organization's drug areas. When we had talked about his priorities for his own role, as we explored his Authentic Leadership Model, it was clear he felt there were some exciting opportunities in the drug field and that he was eager for the company to move into them. I sensed Kevin had a clear vision for how the company might develop to take advantage of new developments.

I found Jimena, the CFO, very impressive, as I had imagined she would be. "Scarily efficient," as Alicia had said, if I was remembering correctly. I noticed that her colleagues tended to refer to her as someone whose judgment they were increasingly relying on—as in, "I spoke to Jimena the other day and she was saying …." She had an encyclopedic knowledge of the company's finances, which also gave her a clear overview of the key drivers of the company's profitability. That's true for any CFO, but in Jimena's case, I sensed a real head for business, in the wider sense, and a firm grasp of what the organization was capable of.

I also noticed a slight wistfulness about people's attitude toward Michael from everyone in the leadership team. It was clear they were still getting time with him, but also that they all felt "it wasn't like the old days." Michael had moved away from them and wasn't quite the mentor they had come to rely on. I could sense an uneasiness in the whole team; a feeling that no one was quite sure who they should turn to anymore and how they all fit into the bigger picture. The effect of Michael's leadership shock was plain to see.

I was at the company's offices for my next meeting with Michael, and I'd arranged to meet Alicia first. She told me she'd been able to do a quick analysis of Michael's calendar with Janet's help and that she had the results ready to show me.

She stood up to greet me as I stepped into her office then sat back down at her desk as I took a seat facing her.

"I've got something to show you," she said, opening her briefcase and taking out a small A4 flip chart presenter with a ring binding. She stood it up on the desk in front of us both.

"Janet and I went through Michael's calendar and did some work," she said. "And we basically found that everything in the calendar fits into one of nine or ten categories."

She opened the black plastic cover of the presenter to reveal the first chart. It was a hand-drawn sketch. In the middle of the page was an entirely recognizable caricature of Michael. Most of the image was of Michael's head, but the artist had sketched a tiny version of his body with a few quick pencil lines. Michael's shirtsleeves were rolled up, his tie loosened, and the top button of his shirt was undone. Alicia had given Michael's cartoon face a bit of an unshaven look, which was unfair, and he looked overwrought—which was not unfair.

Cartoon Michael was surrounded by caricatures of the rest of the team. I could recognize most of them—Jimena, Jeff, Kevin, Gabriela, Alan, Janine from HR—and I guessed the other figure must be the head of research, Benjamin, because he was wearing a scientist's white coat and holding a test tube with some kind of fumes rising from it. Michael's head had been drawn several times, so it looked as if his head was literally spinning as he looked from each of them to the next.

I looked at Alicia quizzically.

"I draw a bit, so I thought I'd liven things up," she said, smiling brightly.

"They're really good!" I said. I meant it.

"Thank you!" said Alicia. "I know this is important to your conversations with Michael, so I thought I'd try to bring it to life for you."

"That's an image that will stick in my mind!" I agreed.

Alicia smiled again.

"I draw really quickly," she said. "It didn't take a moment."

She gestured at the first chart.

"OK. Top team regular meetings and then ongoing involvement on various projects of theirs that Michael basically 'sponsors' and stays with—Janet and I reckon that represents 50 percent of Michael's calendar. At least."

She flipped to the next chart. It was the same image, but, in this version, there were little fires burning next to some of the team.

"Firefighting," said Alicia. "The first 50 percent was the regular meetings and ongoing projects, but there's the emergencies on top. Not many weeks go by without one of the top teams needing urgent attention for something or other. Janet and I reckon another 10 percent for firefighting."

She flipped to the next chart. It was a drawing of Michael's office. The door was open, and inside you could see Michael sitting down with someone who looked like a builder with a hard hat and a high-vis jacket. Outside the door of Michael's office was a long queue of people waiting for his attention, wearing various recognizable outfits: a chef, a gardener, a security guard, a handyman, a cleaner ….

"Office stuff," said Alicia. "You name it. Building projects. Catering. Security. Did I mention the green campus project?"

"You did," I assured her.

"Not much happens in the organization without needing Michael's input. So 'office stuff.' Approving the new furniture for the entrance lobby. Signing off on the new automated voice response to incoming phone calls. Did I mention the green campus project? Oh yeah, I did. That's not my favorite right now." Alicia's voice was rising slightly as it had in our last conversation. "Janet and I reckon 20 percent. About 20 percent of calendar time for office stuff."

It isn't hard to tell when Alicia is getting a little animated. I sensed that the temperature was rising. I nodded.

Alicia flipped the chart.

In front of the logo of the US Food and Drug Administration (FDA), Michael and Benjamin from R&D (still holding his smoking test tube) were facing a panel of serious-looking people seated behind a long desk.

"Approval of new drugs," Alicia said. "Michael stays close to the whole process. Benjamin's team does all the heavy lifting, obviously, but Michael makes a point of keeping close to the whole process, from first idea to approval. He actually does attend important meetings with the FDA. Janet said it was hard to put a figure on how much of Michael's time is involved, because a lot of it is like him popping round to R&D and chatting with people and getting a feel for how it's all going. And a lot of it is covered in routine meetings. But it's a real commitment of his time. We've guessed another 5 percent."

The next image was of Michael in his office shaking hands with someone. Jeff and Kevin were standing beside him.

"External suppliers," said Alicia. "Vendors, contract sales organizations, research, our advertising agencies. Companies that are important to us. Michael meets them all on a regular basis. Not a big consumer of time, but regular. Janet and I think another 5 percent of the calendar."

I nodded again. Alicia flipped the chart.

It was an image of Michael standing at a podium with a microphone.

"External events," said Alicia. "This could be all kinds of stuff. Press briefings, award ceremonies, meetings of professional associations and various committees, charities we support, you name it. Alvin does a lot of that, but he also deputizes to Michael. Five percent."

She flipped the chart.

There was an image of someone sitting in a chair in front of Michael, Jeff, Janine—and Alicia. Alicia's caricature of Alicia looked a lot like Alicia. She'd taken the trouble to put little blobs of scarlet on her cartoon figure's fingernails with a sharpie.

The person in the chair in front of the group looked nervous; there was a bead of perspiration on their forehead.

"Interviews!" said Alicia. "Michael sits in on the final interview for all senior appointments. As do I. It's part of our concern about corporate culture—you know: 'recruit for fit.' We don't make people sweat though, honestly," she said, smiling. "That was just me having fun!"

She glanced away in thought.

"Well, we do make 'em sweat a bit though, you know." She snapped back to the moment. "Anyway, let's say 2.5 percent of Michael's time."

I smiled. Alicia flipped the chart to a picture of what was clearly Alvin sitting at the head of the table in a board meeting. Alvin is tall, Black, and handsome, with a bald head and some distinguished-looking short-cropped gray hair at the sides.

"Alvin and the board," said Alicia. "Michael's always had a weekly meeting with Alvin; that's still in the calendar. But Michael has been spending more time with the board recently and I know he wants to increase that. Let's say 5 percent. It's not 5 percent now but it probably will be soon."

She flipped the chart again. The next was a sketch from a *Peanuts* cartoon of Lucy sitting in her booth with signs saying, "Psychiatric help 5 cents" and "The doctor is IN." Michael's head had been superimposed onto Lucy's cartoon body.

"The open-door policy," said Alicia, a little bitterly. "I know, I know!" she said, looking at me, to forestall criticism I was not about to offer. "It's a wonderful thing. He's a great boss. Anyone can walk into his office and waste his time. I'm sorry, I mean walk into his office and be cherished. We're a cherishing organization. But it takes maybe another 5 percent of his time."

I felt that Alicia may have rolled her eyes a little as she said that, but I was probably mistaken.

"You know I believe in that," Alicia said loudly, as if I had made a comment, which I had not. "I'm the chief of staff. These are my values."

She looked at me as if daring me to contradict her, which I did not.

"It's just that I don't want Michael to die of overwork and stress. Not on my watch."

I felt Alicia may have tossed her head and flared her nostrils a little as she said that, but, again, I was probably mistaken.

She flipped the chart. It was an image of Michael sitting at his desk with his feet up on the desk and his hands behind his head, smiling and looking out the window.

"Zero percent!" said Alicia quite loudly. She said it again. "Zero percent! Michael has no 'me' time. Zero!"

She flipped the chart again. It was an image of the sculpture "The Thinker" by the French sculptor Auguste Rodin. It depicts a seated man, leaning forward with his chin cupped in his hand and his elbow resting on his leg. As with Doctor Lucy, Alicia had superimposed Michael's head on The Thinker's body.

"Thinking time," said Alicia, eyes flashing. "Guess what? Zero!"

She shut the presenter with an emphatic flourish and stared at me with her arms folded.

"Well, you asked," she said, a little triumphantly.

"Thank you," I said. "Genuinely. That's really useful."

"If I'm not mistaken," I said, carefully, "that all adds up to 107.5 percent of Michael's time."

Alicia looked at me in an "Oh, yeah? Do you want to make something of it?" kind of way.

I didn't want to make anything of it. I thanked Alicia warmly again and set off down the corridor to see Michael. As I left, I could see Alicia staring out the window of her office, lost in thought. She had one leg crossed over the other; her free foot was bobbing up and down slightly and her fingernails were drumming on her desk.

I can't say Michael looked any fresher; he still looked tired and drawn. But I'd heard that the interviews for the COO role were now all done, which must have taken some of the strain off Michael's calendar and off him personally. Despite his tiredness, he seemed purposeful and even upbeat. He clearly remembered our last session very well, and we chatted at first about priorities, picking up where we had left off the previous week.

"I've been thinking some more about that," he told me. "And I keep coming back to my vision about growth. I want to achieve all the other things on our list." He ran through the now familiar list of role expectations we had decided on: deliver on performance; give direction to the leadership team; lead for the company within the industry; preserve the culture; lead the organization as a whole; and keep the chairman and the board on side.

"I can deliver on all those fronts," he said, "but if I am not achieving the growth I want and the kind of transformation of the company I want to achieve, then all of those things are a bit meaningless. I mean, we could probably hit the numbers in a different way without the growth. There are some big expenditures built into the next five years that won't deliver that much revenue in the short term. We could strip those out, carry on exactly as normal, and deliver some very healthy figures. It's just that I couldn't do that and live with myself."

He looked at me seriously. I nodded.

"I could deliver on the numbers, but I couldn't genuinely give direction to the leadership team, because I wouldn't be directing them where I want to go. And I could lead within the industry, but I wouldn't be leading the kind of company I think we should be, so I wouldn't get a lot of pleasure out of that. I'd feel a bit of a fraud. And I could safeguard the culture and lead the company as a whole, but actually I want to keep all the good things about our corporate culture but also make us just a bit more adventurous; a bit more swashbuckling."

He looked at me and smiled. In fact, he grinned. That was a first.

"I mean, we don't really do swashbuckling in the pharma business because we're so heavily regulated, which is as it should be, but you know what I mean—I want to take the fight to the big boys a bit more; I want to be a bit of a pirate."

There was a gleam in Michael's eye. I liked his new pirate look.

"And then I've got to take the board with me," said Michael. "But take them where? 'Steady as she goes; business as usual?'"

He scoffed. Michael was getting more and more combative.

"I won't do it," he said.

It was my turn to grin.

"OK," I said. "That's very clear. That's going to feed into everything else we do from now on with your Authentic Leadership Model. Today I'd like to talk about your strengths—or more specifically, the value you feel you bring to the role. I don't have a problem with 'strengths' as a term but this has nothing to do with the Gallup CliftonStrengths program, or StrengthsFinder as it used to be known—you know?"

Michael nodded.

"I mean you've probably done that at some point, right?"

Michael nodded again.

"OK. So any insights you got from that are entirely relevant; I just use 'value I bring' to make it clear that this is very different from the concept of personality assessment. Some aspects of the CliftonStrengths higher-level domains might be relevant—strategic thinking, relationship building, influencing, executing. But what I'm looking for is the specific value you feel you bring to this new role. We've talked about your purpose, the expectations of the role, and your vision and priorities. What would you say is the value you bring to the role that will make you successful?"

Michael sat silent for a while and then, with his customary decisiveness, he began.

"OK. You mentioned 'executing.' I'm very good at getting things done. I'm good at detail, I'm good at perseverance, and I'm good at hard work. And I like problems. So if there's a bit of the business that isn't delivering, you know, some aspect of business process that isn't running as smoothly as it should, I'm good at finding a solution. I'm good at fixing things. And then I think I have good people skills, so I'm very good at helping other people fix things. I don't do so much direct fixing these days. I help the rest of the leadership team surface problems in their own areas and work with them to get those fixed."

I nodded. Michael paused for a while.

"OK, next. I know the industry very well. I know how pharma works, so that helps me run our business, but I also have a very strong network of people across the industry. I know our vendors and suppliers; I know the leadership team of our main competitors; I know the people at the FDA. I know the research organizations. I know the key people in academia—I mean not personally, in general, but I read their work and I know what they're working on. So I think 'knowledge' is part of the value I bring. I bring a lot of knowledge to the role, and I'm plugged into a valuable network."

He paused again.

"I think I'm a good communicator," he said. "I'm good with people one-to-one but I also think I'm good at the set piece stuff. I'm happy on a podium or in front of a camera. I'm happy talking to the press. I'm good at talking to colleagues. I talk to people in the lift, in our cafeteria, and I try to tell them something useful about the company—I tell them what's really important to us right now and what might need special attention. I spread the word."

Michael looked like he might be finished.

"So which of those do you feel are the most significant for your role now?" I asked. "Which of those do you think you can most leverage?"

Michael looked a bit puzzled.

"I think all of them," he said, a little uncertain, which was unusual for him.

"Let me put it another way," I suggested. "Which of those strengths do you feel is the least useful in your current role?"

I could see Michael thinking, and it was taking longer than usual. He didn't reach his typical moment of decisiveness so quickly.

And then he smiled. His shoulders dropped and he looked straight at me.

There is always a moment in the process of working through anyone's Authentic Leadership Model when something falls into place. It's never exactly the same thing because everyone's Authentic Leadership Model is unique to them, but there comes a moment when everything begins to fit together and there can be a light bulb moment.

I sensed Michael was having such a movement.

"I need to stop fixing things," he said, still smiling. "That was a strength in my role as COO. That's what I do. What I used to do," he corrected himself. "But if I keep doing that, I won't get any of the other things done. I need to walk away from that. It's not a strength in the new role, it's a weakness."

I looked at him attentively.

"Everything else works," he said. "I need to use my industry knowledge and my network to help me find the right new partners and the right targets for acquisition. I need to be out telling the press about our new plans and talking up the company's progress. I need to spend more time with individual members of the board, and I need to get Alvin fully on side so he can do a lot of the legwork for me. He's not going to stand in my way, but I need to show him a lot of hard detail before he's fully 'sold.' If we're going to acquire any of the companies I have my eye on, he's going to want all the numbers to show to the board. That's a big job in itself. I'm going to need a team on that."

Michael's mind was racing; I could feel him mentally planning out the next six months.

"I need to help the leadership team fit into their new roles, but I don't need to hold their hands. I need to encourage them to surprise me, and I need to raise their profile within the organization. I want them to be thinking across the whole enterprise, like we said earlier, so I need to get them presenting to the board and I want to help raise their profile outside the company: I want the world to see the talent we have here."

Michael was now beaming.

"But I need to back off the day-to-day stuff."

He looked at me candidly.

"I've been telling myself that it will all get easier once we've appointed a new COO, but that didn't give me any sense of relief, you know? I thought, 'Well, that will lighten some of the load,' but it didn't make me feel any different. It didn't lift the burden. But now I can start to let go."

He fell silent again.

"Thank you," he said finally. "This has been very valuable." He looked like a weight had been lifted from his shoulders.

I told Michael that we needed to move on to the question of *how* he wanted to lead: what his fundamental principles of leadership were—the dos and don'ts of leadership from his perspective—and his core leadership style, the way he wanted to be able to lead. But I felt a hurdle had been crossed. I was certain that Michael had come to see how his old hands-on style of leadership would stand in the way of success in his new role. That he needed to back off from the team and involve himself with different aspects of leadership for the organization.

There was a lot of work still to do, but I felt we were finally on the right path. I thought that Michael's leadership shock might be about to get better.

COREY MUÑOZ

FORMER CHIEF TALENT OFFICER, KPMG LLP

"I think it's human nature to gravitate toward things that you're comfortable with—preferences, all those sorts of things. It's hard to let things go, because those are the things that made you successful. If you're not comfortable with something or not familiar with it, you're going to naturally go back to what you're comfortable with. And for leaders that's often the operational side of things—the execution of tasks, managing work from a project standpoint—and we quickly lose sight of the big picture. We all have a unique value, depending on where we sit in an organization. A lot of times it has to do with access to information: with your purview; the types of meeting you sit in. I think you have to take a step back and say, what is the thing that only I can uniquely do to add value to my team; my organization; my business? I found that that is a helpful frame to think about what you focus on and what you do not. It's hard because it's dynamic. I don't think you can just set a prioritization exercise once a year, I think it's something that you really need to continue to reinforce by reflecting and understanding where your unique value is. You have to make an intentional effort. You have to bring it from the implicit to the explicit. Sometimes it can just be a 10-minute reflection, but sometimes it's more in-depth, where you need to really analyze where you're spending your time, your calendar, all that sort of stuff."

Summary: The Value I Bring

Having a clear understanding of the value you bring to a role is crucially important to the Authentic Leadership Model. In recent years, strengths have become a powerful way for people to think about how they can make an impact on an organization. The Gallup CliftonStrengths assessment (previously known as the Clifton Strengths-

Finder) has become popular and can be very effective. Research has shown that leveraging people's strengths builds community; it helps them feel they are doing good work and helps them to feel fulfilled.

Thinking about your strengths is important. Many leaders who are experiencing leadership shock find that something they are good at that used to be valuable in their previous role is not what they need now. This applies to anyone making their first transition into management. Being the best salesperson or the best engineer is no longer the most important strength they bring to their new role. In their early days as a manager, they may engage with their teams to solve problems and their expertise may still be useful during that phase, but as they move from manager to director to senior director and beyond, their subject matter expertise becomes less important. It will always have value, but it is no longer the most significant value they bring to the role.

We saw this with Michael. His knowledge of how the business runs is no longer the most important value he brings to the CEO role. He has people reporting to him who can run the business. He must reframe what it is that he brings to the table in his new role.

When you are thinking about the value you bring to your current role, it is useful to think about all of the strengths that you bring to the table. These may include things that have not been expressed before and are relatively intangible. It may be that you are a good networker and build good relationships, or that you are good at influencing people; perhaps you are fun to be around. These are all strengths that you might not have thought of as being relevant to your previous roles that could be of great value in your new role.

List all of your strengths and then identify the things that are most important to your current role. Go back to your purpose, your role expectations, and your priorities to test which of all the strengths you've identified are of most value now.

Recognizing the Value You Bring

The value you bring to your role comes from:

- The function of your role within the organization
- Your skills, knowledge, and capabilities
- The skills, knowledge, and capabilities of your team

Value is usually seen under three broad categories:

- Functional expertise
- Management of your team
- Relationships with others, internal and external

Remember:

- The most important values you bring change as you become more senior.
- Your greatest strengths in earlier roles may no longer be the most valuable now.

EXERCISE:

List *all* the strengths you feel you bring to your role.

Identify the *top five* that are most critical to your role.

Remember that some strengths are quite *intangible*: you might be a good networker and good at building relationships; these might be highly valuable in your new role.

Think carefully about what you have always seen as your greatest strengths; are they *still the most valuable*, or do you have other strengths that could bring more value to the new role?

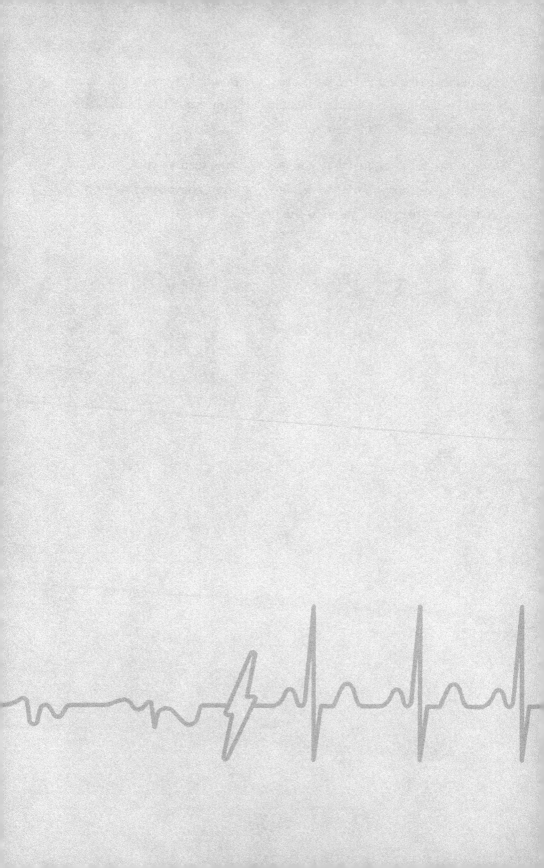

CHAPTER 8

LEADERSHIP BELIEFS

When I next turned up at the company's office, there was a sense of panic in the air. As I walked into Michael's office, Janet quickly got up and pulled me to one side.

"Jeff's been taken ill," she told me in an urgent whisper. "He's been taken into a hospital."

Janet told me how Jeff had been presenting at a meeting when he collapsed suddenly into a chair and doubled up, clutching his abdomen. He had been feeling unwell for some days, talking about feelings of nausea, a temperature, and vague stomach pains. Now he was clearly in distress. Alicia, who had been in the same meeting, had been the hero of the hour. Jeff had insisted he was fine, and it was probably just food poisoning, but Alicia had insisted on getting him to an urgent care center, driving him there herself after getting colleagues to help Jeff out the building, where she was waiting with the car. The urgent care center diagnosed acute appendicitis and had Jeff rushed to the ER in an ambulance. Alicia had visited in the evening when Jeff was beginning to come round after his general anesthetic. Michael had gone with her.

"He's doing fine," Janet told me. "But it was a close call. The hospital says his appendix could have ruptured anytime. We're all a bit shaken up."

It was a few days before I could see Michael again. He looked serious and a bit distracted, but somehow less stressed. I sensed some big decisions had been taken.

"How's it going?" I asked.

"We're OK," he said carefully. "We're all a bit worried about Jeff, but he's going to be fine. We all owe a lot to Alicia."

He glanced at me, smiling.

"I mean, no change there, right? But she quite possibly saved Jeff's life. He was brushing the whole thing off, saying it was probably just food poisoning and he'd be fine, but Alicia took control and got him straight to the hospital. She was right. In another hour or so it could have been full-blown peritonitis."

"But he's doing OK?"

"He's actually fine. It took him a couple of days to recover after the operation, but now he's home. Panic over."

"I'm so glad," I said. "It must be very unsettling for everyone."

"Well, thank you," Michael said. "We're a pretty close-knit team, so, yes."

We chatted for a while about the incident and then got down to business.

"How are things with Alvin?" I asked.

Michael looked at me quizzically.

"Why do you ask?"

"I just thought, after our last few meetings, there might have been some developments," I said.

Michael looked at me as if he thought I was a witch. Or a wizard. Or whatever.

"Uh, well, we've had some interesting conversations," he said finally. "I think we've reached some important agreements."

We talked about Michael's recent interactions with Alvin. Michael talked about it very diplomatically, but I sensed there had been some serious differences of opinion and that Michael had needed to be quite forceful, but the strong bond between the two of them was still very much in evidence.

"Alvin and I have a fundamental disagreement about the way forward," Michael told me. "I am convinced, like I said, that we need to buy in new developments. That we need to acquire new molecules that some specialist firms are developing, which probably means acquiring the firms, and then, more significantly, that we need to buy in what would effectively be a whole new division in a new drug area by acquiring some smaller competitors. Maybe mergers, but I'm thinking more of acquisitions. Probably several acquisitions. Alvin is all in favor of growth, but he's pretty wedded to the organic route. Sorry, I told you that already."

Michael glanced at me apologetically.

"I understand where he's coming from," Michael went on. "He worries about diluting or even changing our corporate culture, which is a fair point. So do I. But I think the organic route is too slow. We need to get bigger fast. I'm worried about us becoming an acquisition target ourselves. We need to get too big to swallow. We need to convince our shareholders that we have a bright future and they're better off leaving us in control than seeing us vanish into one of the big outfits."

Michael's eyes were clear, and he talked firmly and confidently.

"But I think I've brought Alvin round to my way of thinking. He's too good a boss to try to stop me doing what I'm sure is right for us. And he wouldn't have given me the job if he thought I was wrong. So Alvin's been laying out his side of the argument very strongly and I've been pushing back. We've reached an agreement. I've persuaded Alvin that I'm right. Which wasn't easy, actually."

He glanced at me.

"Alvin knows what my plans are. I spelt them out in detail in the interviews for the CEO role. But it's different now he sees them about to happen in reality. It's not the route he would have chosen himself and he's struggling with it. I think it was the first time Alvin realized he wasn't CEO anymore."

He looked at me again, and I nodded. I was starting to feel like a very happy man.

"But now he's accepted it, he's going to help me sell my ideas to the board, which is hugely important."

"How is the new COO appointment going?" I asked.

Michael drew a deep breath and gave a wry smile.

"Well, that's something else Alvin and I seem to be disagreeing on. I mean, we used to be pretty much of the same mind on that front, but I think I've had a change of heart."

He looked at me in a strange sort of way. I wondered what I had done.

"It's probably no secret that Jimena is the front-runner for the COO role," he said.

He looked at me inquiringly. I put on my best poker face, but I knew if anyone in the company was running a book on who was going to be the next COO, Jimena would have the shortest odds. Michael put me out of my misery.

"Well, she is the front-runner," he said. "And I have to say I am a big supporter. I keep an open mind about all the candidates, but Jimena has great strengths. But there was a moment in the interviews …."

He broke off and looked at me searchingly again. I had definitely done something wrong. I racked my brains to think what it could be.

"All the internal candidates talked about the value they bring to the role. And they used those exact words, so I know you've been working your magic on their Authentic Leadership Models."

He smiled. I didn't think that was the thing I had done wrong.

"And they talked about their various strengths, and they all have a compelling case to make. But Kevin said something that really made me think."

Kevin was the head of marketing. I did find him very impressive, and I had enjoyed working with him on his leadership model.

"Kevin said that going through his Authentic Leadership Model with you had made him think about his goals as a leader and his leadership style. About where he wanted to spend his time and how he wanted to lead. Which, if I may say so, sounds like classic Steinberg."

Steinberg is me: Pete Steinberg. I began to think maybe I hadn't done anything wrong after all.

"Kevin said the process made him aware of how he approached leadership and made him realize that he would need to change if he was given the COO role. He was basically telling us that he had various great strengths, et cetera, but he realized he would have to operate differently as COO—which was something he was very much up for. And he talked about the new directions the company might move in and his own vision for drug areas we should be exploring, and …"

Another searching look at me.

"And I began to think that Kevin might be our man."

In my mind I was out of my seat again, doing a victory lap of Michael's office and high-fiving the same team of imaginary team members. I mean, I do have real team members, they're not imaginary, but they weren't actually in Michael's office with me. You know what I mean.

I wasn't mentally celebrating because it looked like Michael had chosen Kevin for the COO role. I was happy for Michael to appoint whoever he thought was the best candidate. What was exciting was that my work on the Authentic Leadership Model with Kevin had given Kevin the metacognition we'd talked about. He was thinking about how he went about the process of leadership and how that might have to change if he was given a new leadership challenge. And Michael could see that Kevin had successfully been through that process with me. And Michael was beginning to come out of his own leadership shock and be able to reset his priorities and decide where he should be spending his time. It was all working. I hadn't done anything wrong; I had done everything right.

Michael was still looking at me.

"I think you have helped a lot in this process, Pete," he said. "I think you've helped me focus on what's important and what I have to prioritize going forward, and it's clear you're helping the team also. So, thank you."

I mumbled some form of thanks and said it was nothing … all in a day's work, etc., etc. But internally, I was still doing my mental victory lap. It felt good.

"Now," said Michael suddenly, bringing me instantly back into sharp focus. "I'm not saying that Jimena didn't demonstrate that she was going through a similar process, because she is. She absolutely has the capacity to change and take on these new challenges. And she's a person of immense importance to the future of this company. I'm just beginning to feel that Kevin is more up for change. He is up for some disruption. In fact, he seemed eager for it. Jimena is a bit more, you know, conservative."

He glanced at me again, but I had my poker face back on again. I wasn't giving anything away. It wasn't that I disagreed with him about Jimena, I was just struggling to stop myself from doing a little dance right there in the office.

"Jimena is absolutely on top of everything, you know?" said Michael.

I allowed myself to nod in agreement.

"But that means she's not a huge fan of change. She likes everything to stay the way she knows it and likes it. Which is probably why Alvin was so much in favor of Jimena for the COO role."

It looked to me as if that was the first time Michael had actually articulated that thought to himself.

We went on to talk about the thing we had been scheduled to talk about that session: Michael's personal leadership approach.

All leaders have their own distinctive leadership styles that they have settled into, and which have served them well in their career to date. The Authentic Leadership Model allows us to decide whether our role expectations, our vision, our priorities, and the value we bring to a role are actually best served by our preferred leadership style. It helps leaders decide where they should spend their time and how they should spend their time, and, most importantly, it helps them decide exactly how they want to lead, because the way they have led up till now might not be how they should lead in their new role. Clinging unthinkingly to the "old" leadership style can be a big part of leadership shock. It can be one of the main reasons why everything seems to stop working all of a sudden.

It could be that your "instinctive" leadership approach is to lead from the front in a directive way. You might define a leader as "someone who takes people where they wouldn't normally go" and see your main function as bringing about change that wouldn't happen without your input.

Another view of leadership might be a variation on servant leadership, where a leader sees their main function as enabling the team, helping them to carry out their role as well as they are able so the team delivers its overall objective. You might define a leader as "someone who offers support and helps people be their best selves" and see your main function as setting the overall objective, ensuring the team has the tools they need to do the job and helping to clear any obstacles that lie in their way.

Other leaders see their main role as being "communicator in chief." They set the vision and then use every opportunity to communicate that vision all the way through the organization. Others might see themselves as a kind of "shepherd": they don't think it's appropriate in their organization that they should overtly direct people and tell them what to do, but they have a clear vision for where the organization should be headed and what people need to do to get to that place, so they nudge people in the right direction. There are many leadership approaches, and this is not the place to discuss their relative merits. Most leaders display their own unique mix of different approaches. The most important thing is that leaders come to a fuller understanding of what their leadership approach is—the one that has served them so well to date—because this instinctive approach can clash with their new priorities and guiding principles about how they should lead their team. I tend to ask people what they believe is great leadership. Then

I explore why they hold those beliefs, to introduce that vital element of "metacognition." People often start to modify their beliefs in the course of this discussion, and then we test their current behavior against these modified beliefs to see if they are living up to them.

I talked Michael through some of these ideas and asked him about how he saw his own approach to leadership. "I think I'm primarily a servant leader," Michael told me as soon as I had posed the question. "I know what we want to achieve, I make sure the team all understand it, and I help them deliver their part of it. I'm the guy who fixes things, who helps everyone get over the hurdles that get in the way of their success. I'm a big fan of helping people be their best. I don't need to be up on my high horse waving a banner. I steer people in the right direction and get things done. It works."

I nodded.

"That teamwork emerged very strongly in your purpose," I reminded him. "Working as a team to make a difference in people's lives."

It was Michael's turn to nod.

"That's very powerful," I said. "That's what energizes you and fills your tank. From everything you've told me, I can't see you being fulfilled by any kind of solitary achievement; I think you need to feel you're leading a team to achieve something. And that 'something' has to make a difference, and I think in your case it has to be quite a tangible difference. You know, I'm happy with the idea that all human activity makes a difference in some way, but I think you get a lot out of the big things—curing illness, making people's lives better. And then you have this other powerful instinct toward servant leadership; toward helping other people achieve the goals you all share and be the best they can be."

Michael nodded.

"But what about your new role as CEO? How do you see your role for the next, let's say, three years? What kind of leadership approach is going to get the organization to where you want it to be?"

There was a long silence. I had gotten to know Michael well enough to know that this was an interesting sign.

"'Instinct' is a good word," he said finally.

I raised an eyebrow inquiringly.

"It's my instinct to help the team achieve our goals. I'm not going to stop doing that. I don't think I'm going to be able to stop myself from doing that."

He glanced at me.

"But I need to bring about some major change. I'm going to do what I can to help everyone play their part in that …"

He stopped himself. He was silent for a few more moments.

"Or maybe I'm not going to do that," he said finally.

He stared at me.

"Maybe I'm going to have to be a lot more of a figurehead. Maybe I need the horse and the banner. I have a very clear vision of where we need to get to, and I need everyone to share that vision. But there's a lot of decisions to be made that only I can take. I mean, I need everyone's input, but only I can make the decision at the end of the day—like which companies we target for acquisition and which ones we actually buy. And when the decision has been taken there's going to be a ton of work to be done, and I need other people to be doing that work so I can move on to the next target. So I need to be a lot less hands-on, but I need to be very visible. I need everyone in the organization to know why we're doing things and what comes next. I'm going to need to do a lot of communicating. And a lot of that is going to be communicating with the board, with Alvin's help."

He paused.

"You're right," he said finally. "My instincts are not going to serve me well. I need to lead from the front, pull people with me, and leave it to other people to do the hand holding and the fixing. Like maybe Kevin."

He looked at me and actually grinned.

"Kevin will not complain," I said. "He's up to the task. What about Jimena?"

"I want Jimena on board, but not in her old role," he said decisively. "I need her financial smarts. I mean, I need them personally, not for the company. There's a whole bunch of number crunching that's going to come with every planned acquisition, and I want Jimena leading that. I don't want her distracted by the day-to-day stuff. I need her to be able to do the numbers on a whole range of strategic options. I want her to report directly to me, alongside Kevin. I'm thinking of maybe 'Head of Strategic Finance.'"

He looked at me inquiringly.

"Sounds good to me," I said. "Do you think Jimena would be happy with the role?"

"I think she'll find it a wrench to move away from the core finances. There's a very real sense in which Jimena helps to run this company. She knows what makes everything tick. She was like my wingman. Whatever we did, I knew the finances were taken care of and made sense. But I need her to help me take the company in a new direction. I think she'll welcome that challenge. I hope so. I'd hate to lose her."

"And Kevin?"

"Well, he's going to love the COO role. And I don't think it would work for Jimena to be reporting to him. I don't think it would be fair on either of them. Kevin can get his own CFO with Jimena's input and build a relationship with them."

"Sounds like a plan," I said.

"Kevin's right," said Michael. "He's going to face a whole new leadership challenge. And it won't even be the same challenges I faced, because the job will get bigger and there will be a lot of change to be absorbed. He's going to need his Authentic Leadership Model!"

"The good news is that the Authentic Leadership Model isn't static," I said. "It's a framework. If he thinks about his purpose and where he should be spending his time and the way he wants to lead, he'll be fine."

"How's Jeff?" I asked as I was about to leave.

"I went to see him in the hospital again," said Michael, "and he was in good shape. He needs a few weeks off to recover. I'm going to go round to his place in the next few days, after I've spoken to Kevin and Jimena but before I make any announcement, so I can talk him through it personally. I'm not saying it was never going to be Jeff, but he's not the COO we need right now. I think he'll understand. And I need him to know it has nothing to do with this illness. He'll be fighting fit in no time. But he'll probably use the appendicitis against me. 'You're not appointing me just because I got sick. That's completely unfair. I demand a rematch!' Jeff doesn't miss a trick, you know?"

He smiled at me.

"I gather Alicia really helped out when he was taken ill," I said. "I didn't think she was Jeff's biggest fan."

Michael smiled gently.

"What you need to know about Alicia is that she is fiercely loyal, with a pretty strict hierarchy of loyalties," he said. "So if, for example, there was a terrorist attack on the company and we were all being held at gunpoint, Alicia would kill the people who were threatening Alvin first, and then, I think ..."

He looked a bit embarrassed.

"And then I think she'd kill the people threatening me. And then she'd do what she could for everyone else. I wouldn't give much for the terrorist's chances, by the way."

"I know what you mean," I said.

"But Alicia's got everyone's back. She thinks Jeff has been too demanding of my time, especially lately, so she gives him a hard time. Doesn't mean she doesn't love him really."

COREY MUÑOZ
FORMER CHIEF TALENT OFFICER, KPMG LLP

"I think that your leadership style has to be rooted in your values and your motives and your purpose as an individual. We all have experiences that we have gained through the years, both positive and negative, even before our working lives. You have to sit down and bring that from somewhere in the back of your mind to the forefront and then say, 'OK, because of this, I'm going to lead in a certain way.' But you have to know what that is. It's like your leadership DNA.

"A lot of leaders don't view their leadership style as something that they need to take a step back and reflect on and think about how their leadership needs to evolve and change. What often happens is they learn it eventually, but it takes way too long, and they have a lot of bumps and bruises along the way to get it right. I think it's somewhere where personal values, motives, and purpose—I don't know what word would make the most sense—intersect with how that translates into the type of leader that they want to be. How do they exhibit those things? How do they reinforce that value system through their leadership?

"For me, it's about really understanding your own personal values. And sometimes, you know, a leader has never done that. They've been in leadership roles for twenty years, and they'll recite the firm's values, or their business principles or something like that. But it's a much more personal thing that takes reflection; it takes time for you to step away. But I think it's so critical for people to lead from that; to understand their core beliefs and values and make that congruent with their leadership behaviors and style.

"The other part that is a challenge for leaders is obviously we've all built styles, we've had things in our toolbox that have been very successful for us, and those things don't always translate as you move up and move into different roles. I think the people part is probably one of the most common that people underestimate. Because if you're a new leader, it's easy to fall into the trap of 'I need to come up with an amazing strategy; I need to have a killer idea!' So you over-index on that. But really, the power is in how you're leading and motivating and developing your team. We all underestimate that. As a manager, that looks a certain way, but as a C-suite executive that looks a completely different way. And I think people always underestimate that."

Summary: Leadership Beliefs

The Authentic Leadership Model is grounded in things you believe.

Your purpose—the starting point of the model—is critical and is likely to be relatively fixed. It may change over a long period of time, but probably not by very much. The leadership model is also grounded in your vision, which is an account of the things you most want to achieve and is dynamic and should always be changing. Another important authentic aspect of the model is your beliefs about leadership.

What do you believe makes a good leader? What is it that you believe good leaders do?

There is no right or wrong answer because everyone is different. When I teach workshops on leadership, I tell the leaders I work with that for any question they have about leadership, the answer will be: "It depends." It depends on the context, and it depends on the leader.

We all develop beliefs about what constitutes good leadership through our own experience and through our education and wider reading. It is very easy to acquire certain ideas about what good leadership is and what good leaders do, but then find, on reflection, that you don't actually think those things are a central part of your own leadership style.

When you are developing your leadership beliefs, you might find these three things useful. First, write down something that you think is true about successful leadership. Now write down why that is an important attribute that a leader brings to the table. Finally, write down why you think that attribute is important for good leadership. It's that third, metacognitive question, reflecting on why you hold that belief, that is most important. At this point, you will know if this is a true leadership belief you hold.

An example might be that you include "giving good feedback" in your list of things that good leaders do. And you say that giving good feedback is important because it helps a team to improve. But when you reflect on why you think that attribute is important, you might find yourself thinking that is something you instinctively do as a manager—that one of your strengths as a manager is providing feedback to the team so they can improve—but that is not a critical aspect of your leadership.

You might decide that creating a culture of feedback is more significant for a leader. Creating a culture of feedback is different from giving feedback. Giving feedback tends to be something that a manager does. Creating a culture of feedback is something a leader does. Perhaps "creating a culture of feedback" should be on your initial list of what successful leaders do.

Work through the list, reflect on it, and decide on what aspects of your leadership are most significant to your current role and most likely to help you achieve your vision.

Exploring Your Leadership Beliefs

Think about what you believe makes a good leader.

This might include:

- Mindset

- Skills

- Attributes

Every leader is different. All leadership depends on context and the leaders themselves.

We develop beliefs over time about the attributes of great leadership. It is crucial to reflect on why we hold those beliefs.

Most people would say that George Washington was a great leader. Do you agree?

What important leadership attributes do you feel he had?

Examples of leadership beliefs:

- Great leaders lead from the front to set expectations.

- Great leaders set the vision to enable alignment.

- Great leaders empower the team by explicitly giving them decision rights.

- Great leaders encourage innovation by providing time and supporting mistakes.

EXERCISE:

Make a list of people you think of as great leaders.

- What do you think are the most *important attributes* of their leadership?

- *Why* do you think they are the important attributes for those leaders?

- Do you think they are important attributes for *all* leaders?

This is your list of leadership beliefs. We will come back to this later in the model when we think about your leadership principles.

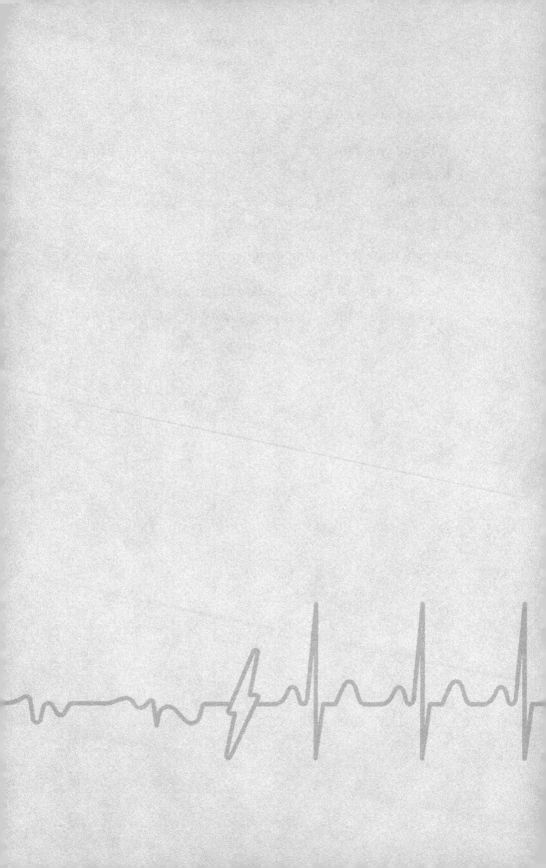

CHAPTER 9

LEADERSHIP PRINCIPLES

It was a few weeks before I saw Michael again. He had talked to Kevin and Jimena and then announced the new appointments to the whole company, arranging an off-site meeting for every employee at a local hotel.

I caught up with Alicia on Zoom a few days later.

"Pete! How are you doing?" she said. She looked radiant.

"I'm good, thank you. How's it all been?"

"Where do I start?"

"Well—how was the big announcement?"

"It was really good, honestly," said Alicia. She looked like she meant it.

"I mean, Kevin's appointment was a bit of a shock, you know? We all thought it was going to be Jimena. But I think it's clever. Kevin will be great, and I think Jimena is genuinely excited."

"Have you talked to her?"

"Obviously!" she fired back. "I mean, just for like a few hours over a few cocktails! She really wanted the COO role, but I think she can see the logic. And I think maybe deep down she's actually happy. This way she's on the top team, in a kind of triumvirate with Michael and Kevin. And she gets to do what she loves doing: playing with financial scenarios; shaping the future of the company. I think she's a bit nervous, to be honest, because this is a big challenge and it's very different from just running a tight ship. But I think she's going to love it."

"And Kevin?"

"Over the moon, obviously. He gave a great talk at the off-site. Very inspirational, about all the potential there is and how good the future can be, picking up on what Michael laid out about his vision. Jimena was great too—very upbeat."

"Are you happy?" I asked.

"I am, I really am," she said earnestly. "I would have liked it to be Jimena for COO, but, genuinely, I can see where Michael's coming from. And I think Kevin will be great."

"What's the general mood in the company like?" I asked.

"Oh, it's good. It's really good. You know, change is always scary, but this just feels like change for the better. We've still got Alvin and Michael, and now we've got Kevin and Jimena and then their replacements. And there's going to be growth. New jobs, new opportunities. It's scary, but it's great. Everyone's very energized."

"How's Alvin?" I asked.

Alicia paused for a little longer than usual.

"He's OK," she said finally.

I raised my questioning eyebrow.

"I think he's still getting used to not being CEO, you know? He gave a great talk, and he literally got a standing ovation. Everyone loves Alvin. And he looked proud and happy about the new team. But I just sense he misses not being in the driving seat. I mean, chairman's pretty important, right?"

She glanced at me.

"Pretty important," I agreed. "Like, lead the board, focus on strategy, be the face of the business, ensure good governance. Big job."

"Yeh," said Alicia. "I just think ..."

I waited.

"It's just that Michael's doing all this stuff now, you know? Michael's in the chair now. Well, he's not 'the chair,' but you know what I mean. Michael's calling the shots and making the big decisions. And Alvin will do whatever it takes to get Michael's ideas through the board. But ... you know?"

"He'll settle into it," I said. "He's going to have plenty of new challenges. You wouldn't mind being chairperson, right?"

She laughed. "Well, you know, we all have to make sacrifices! Sometimes you have to leave the job you love to take on new responsibilities. Duty calls!"

"I'm going to remind you of that when you are chairperson of some organization," I said. "It's only a matter of time."

I wasn't kidding. I could have sworn Alicia blushed a little.

"How's Jeff?" I asked. "I'm told you saved his life."

Alicia definitely blushed a little.

"Oh, it was nothing," she said untruthfully. "Jeff was being his usual stubborn self."

She clutched her stomach, leaned forward, and did a passable imitation of Jeff in great pain, struggling to talk. She dropped her voice half an octave and groaned: "Just a stomach bug. Nothing to see here. Not dying or anything! No reason to make a fuss."

"So, we dragged his sorry ass out of there ..."

She glanced at me and pulled an apologetic face.

I smiled.

"We dragged him out of there to my car and I got him to the local urgent care center. No big deal. But, as it happens, I was right, you know? Appendix about to explode any moment. Not amusing!"

Alicia's voice had risen that familiar semitone. She looked at me as if I was about to argue with her. I was not.

"But you don't even like Jeff," I said—a little mischievously, I'll admit.

"Oh, I could happily strangle him sometimes," she said. "But only because he's a pain in the …." She checked herself. "Only because he can be kind of annoying sometimes, you know?" She smiled sweetly. "But it wouldn't be personal. I mean, there'd be the whole homicide angle, but it wouldn't be because I don't like the guy. He's one of us. No one gets left behind. You know what I mean?"

I did.

"How's Michael's calendar?"

She looked at me and laughed.

"Ah-ha! This is kind of where you came in, right?"

"Pretty much."

"Well, it's not fixed yet, but it doesn't matter anymore, you know? Michael's back on it. He knows what he's doing. He's winding down his regular meetings and starting to hand over to Kevin. He's huddling with Jimena and Alvin talking about acquisitions. He keeps telling us to drop stuff from his calendar, actually. You know, Janet reminds him he has an appointment, and he just says, 'Oh, leave it to Kevin' or 'Jeff can handle that.' Or sometimes, 'Ah, that's really important, yeah, I'll be there.' We know what we're doing again, you know?"

When I met Michael for what would be one of our final sessions, he looked like a different man. He looked destressed and confident. I guessed I was seeing the "pre-leadership shock" Michael for the first time.

"How's things?" I asked.

"Pretty good, actually. Feeling good."

He literally beamed. I smiled happily.

"OK," I said. "Let's get going. We're nearly at the end of your leadership model."

Michael looked a little surprised.

"Don't worry," I said. "After today's session we'll draw up a graphic representation of your leadership model together, for you to refer to in the future. But remember that the model is a methodology, not a one-off solution. If you recall the process we went through here, it will get you through any future leadership challenge. You won't need to employ me again. I'm not like a leadership coach who needs to be always on hand. Once we're done here, we're done."

Michael looked at me and smiled.

"I think that's arguably poor salesmanship, Pete," he said.

"Tell me about it!" I said, smiling.

"In our early sessions we focused on *where* you should spend your time," I began. "The expectations of your role, your vision for the role, your priorities. The stuff you need to get done. In the last few sessions, we've been focused more on *how* you should spend your time. On the value you bring to the role and your leadership approach. You said in our last session you thought your previous instinctive leadership approach wasn't going to be appropriate for the new role. That maybe you would need to be less of an enabler and more of a figurehead; more 'leading from the front.' Is that fair?"

Michael nodded.

"Can I go back a bit to the *where* you were spending your time while you were COO?" I asked. "I think it might be useful."

"Sure!" said Michael.

"Alicia and Janet did an analysis of your calendar," I said.

Michael pulled a face but managed a wry smile.

"That was not a fun time."

Sadly, I hadn't asked Alicia for her visuals because they were just for my benefit. I wished I had, because I could use them now. But I had my notes.

"They reckoned about 50 percent of your time was spent on regular meetings and ongoing projects you were 'sponsoring' and staying with over time. Then there was an additional 10 percent of time spent in the same areas but on emergencies: on firefighting. You remember that diagram: top-right quadrant, ablaze—urgent?"

"I do remember," said Michael, smiling. He seemed to be all smiles that day.

"How do you feel about that aspect of your calendar now?" I asked.

Michael had a one-word answer.

"Kevin," he said.

"The next 20 percent of your calendar was what I think Alicia called 'office stuff': building projects, catering, security. I think she mentioned the green campus project?"

Michael smiled a little more self-consciously.

"Well, I'd like to say 'Kevin,' because I am going to leave most of that stuff to him, but, actually, I think the green campus project is important, so I'm going to stay with that. And I'm never going to be absent from, you know, catering, security, and stuff. Making sure we offer people a good place to work. But that will be through my regular interactions with Kevin."

"OK. Drug approval process, 5 percent," I continued.

Michael leaned forward.

"I'd like to think it was always more than that," he said. "Anyway. Critical importance. Major shift of focus. I will clear more of my calendar for that."

"And I'm guessing that acquisitions will be a new focus of your calendar from now on?"

"Yes, indeed," he agreed.

"External suppliers," I continued, reading from my notes. "Vendors, contract sales organizations, research, advertising agencies."

"Hm," said Michael. "I mean—not so much. Some key people, maybe."

"External events. Press briefings, awards ceremonies, professional associations, charities."

"Yes," said Michael. "Some of those are now down to Kevin, some of them may still be down to Alvin. Some of them I should definitely do."

I worked on down the list.

"Interviews. Sitting in on final interviews for key appointments."

"Some," said Michael. "Only those where Kevin wants my input."

"The board," I said. "Alicia and Janet estimated maybe 5 percent of your time was spent on reacting with the board."

"A lot more going forward," said Michael. "Maybe 10 percent. We'll see."

"And finally," I said, "open-door policy. Not Alicia's favorite. Maybe 5 percent."

Michael smiled again. "Not going to change!"

It was my turn to smile.

"So how are you feeling about your calendar?" I asked.

"Like a massive weight has been lifted off my shoulders," he replied quickly. "I was always going to appoint a COO—obviously," he said. "And I was always going to pass on a lot of the workload to them—also obviously. But it wasn't freeing up my mind. I didn't feel like I was going to be able to let go of anything, even when we had a new COO in place. Now I do. Now I feel I know where my focus needs to be."

"And finally," I said, "Alicia mentioned 'me' time and thinking time. The chance for you to get some time to yourself and do some reflecting."

Michael snorted derisively.

"Well, yes," I said. "I can imagine there wasn't much opportunity for that. But that might be even more important now?"

"I think so," said Michael seriously, after a pause. "I mean, I do a lot of my thinking in conversation with other people, so I'll be thinking with Kevin, with Jimena, with Alvin. But I wouldn't say no to some thinking time all to myself. Also, maybe I can spend some time with my family now, you know? I've been pretty absent. I can spend some time thinking in my garden. That would be nice."

"I would seriously recommend that you block out some 'me' time in your calendar," I said. "Create some blank spaces. Get Janet to make sure you get home early a certain number of days per week. Make sure your calendar isn't literally full, from dawn till dusk. Spend some time with the family. Sit in the garden."

"That would be nice," agreed Michael.

I returned to the business of the day.

"I think we can see *where* you need to spend your time in your new role," I said. "I think that's become much clearer. Let's get back to the *how* of, 'how you want to spend your time.' We need to talk about your leadership principles. These can be a little difficult because they're not obvious at first glance. But if we get them right, they will help you in every decision you make. You'll be able to think, 'Does this fit with my leadership principles?' And that will help you take the right action."

Michael looked interested.

"We've established your vision and your priorities," I began.

Michael nodded.

"And we talked last time about 'how you want to lead,' which was interesting."

"Yes," said Michael. "I haven't settled into that yet, to be honest, but I'm looking forward to it. Less enablement, more leading from the front. More showing people where we can get to."

"Your leadership principles are the things that need to be true about your approach to leadership for you to be able to implement your priorities and your vision," I said.

I could see Michael reflecting on that.

"I think I'm going to need an example," he said.

"Well, let's take the idea of enabling people," I suggested. "Most leaders want to enable their senior team. A lot of leaders say they want to empower people to make decisions, and they suggest this might be a leadership principle. But it's not really a leadership principle, it's an outcome that they want. They want people to be empowered. A *principle* might be, 'People will be empowered if they understand the strategy.' Because if they genuinely understand the strategy, they can work out for themselves what part of the business can contribute to achieving the strategy. So now they're really empowered. They can make their own decisions, confident that they are moving things in the right direction. Another way of expressing that leadership principle is, 'Whenever I talk to the team, I talk about strategy.' Does that make sense?"

"It does," said Michael, a bit hesitant. "I'm still thinking about what my own principles would be."

"We'll come to those in a moment, if I may," I said. "I think, if we stay with this example for a moment, you can see there are three levels of statement: 'I want to empower people to make decisions'; 'People will be empowered if they understand the strategy'; and 'Whenever I talk to the team, I talk about strategy.'"

Michael nodded in a "I'm still processing it" kind of way.

"I would say that if a statement starts with 'I want …,' it's not really a leadership principle," I continued. "It's an outcome we want to achieve. It's an expectation of behavior. The other two statements *are* leadership principles, but they're different, because one is a kind of pure principle: 'People will be empowered if they understand the strategy.'"

"That's a principle you could use to inform your decisions," I said, looking at Michael. "You might be thinking what is the best course of action that will stay true to your approach to leadership and allow you to implement your priorities and your vision, and if you think to yourself, 'People will be empowered if they understand the strategy,' that would guide you to making the right decision."

Michael pursed his lips thoughtfully. I kept going.

"The other is more like a call to action: 'Whenever I talk to the team, I talk about strategy.' That's something you should always do, so use that as a reminder for yourself."

Michael began to look more engaged.

"We don't need to obsess over the detail of this," I said. "About whether something is an expectation of behavior or a pure leadership principle or a call to action. What we need to get to is a set of principles that you're comfortable with, that can help change your behavior in the future so that you achieve your priorities and your vision. Things you can use as a guide. They need to be memorable. They need to be something you can use as a quick mental checklist when you're wondering if what you are doing is genuinely following your current leadership model."

Michael nodded decisively.

We started to talk about his vision and his priorities.

"The vision is simple, really," said Michael. "Like we said, I want to see the company grow substantially, through organic growth but also through a substantial acquisition program, but without changing our corporate culture in any way. We still stay exactly who we've always been, just bigger."

I nodded.

"The priorities are becoming more and more clear. Growth is the key priority, and acquisitions are a huge part of that. There's a big chunk of work to be done right there. So that's a priority. And then I want to empower the team—the things we've just been talking about—but I don't want to be such an enabler, a Mr. Fixit. I haven't got time and it's not the right thing to do. I want them to genuinely run their own businesses and do whatever they feel they need to do to achieve our objectives. I want them to surprise me, not just deliver exactly what I ask."

He paused.

"I also want to help them develop. I want an ongoing leadership development plan for each of them that will help them grow as leaders, and I want to raise their profile with the board. I want them coming to board meetings and presenting their own plans and achievements rather than me reporting on that for them. I want the board to get to know them, who they are, and what they do. And, by the way ..."

He looked at me over his glasses.

"I fully expect to lose some of them along the way. If someone doesn't get approached to head up some other operation, then I'm not doing my job right. I have to acknowledge that's a price we may have to pay, but hopefully we'll be in a place that keeps attracting the best talent, because people will be able to see where a career with us can take them."

Another pause.

"I think the other priorities are probably embedded in the things we've already talked about," Michael said. "Maintain the corporate culture. That's a huge priority. Bring everyone along with us. That's also huge. Help everyone see how the new development will build a better company and give them a better future; make it personal."

He glanced at me.

"You know you said that 'I want' was not a good leadership principle? Well, I find those easier. I think the big 'I wants' for me are, I want everyone to understand where we are going and why. I want everyone to buy into that—which will take time. But it's one thing to understand where we're going; in an ideal world I want everyone in the company to be happy about where we're going. I want everyone to see what's in it for them—that when we do all these things, it will mean a more secure and better life for them and their families. And communicating all those things successfully is my biggest task. My main priority. Because otherwise we won't be successful; we won't achieve the growth I want. So I need to think about those 'I wants' and turn them into principles."

He leaned back.

"I like it," I said. "As I said, you and I need to spend a last piece of time drawing up your Authentic Leadership Model, so I'm going to ask you to put words under each of the key headings: Purpose, Vision,

Role Expectation, Value I Bring, Approach to Leadership, Priorities, and, then finally, Leadership Principles."

"But my first suggestion for principles that might come out of those 'I wants' might be something like, 'Communicating the vision leads to alignment and inspiration.'"

Michael looked thoughtful; I went on.

"How about, 'Explaining the outcomes creates buy-in from the whole organization'? And maybe, 'Giving people a reason to believe leads to commitment.' And perhaps, 'Making the team leaders of their own businesses creates real empowerment.' Or you could turn some of those into actions: 'Whenever I talk to the organization, I am going to talk about the outcomes of our new developments.' How am I doing?"

"Not bad for starters," Michael said, smiling broadly. "Leave it with me. I'll make a start at drawing up my leadership model with some new leadership principles and then I'd be grateful for the chance to talk that through with you next time."

"My pleasure," I said. "I think we're almost done."

I don't want to sound overdramatic, but when I finish working on a client's Authentic Leadership Model, I always feel a sense of loss; it's a bit like bereavement. You work very intensely with someone for maybe six months and get to know them very well. You get to know what makes them tick as a person. I'm not a psychotherapist, but you do get to share people's hopes and dreams and you get to know their strengths and their weaknesses—at least in terms of their work. And because their work is so central to who they are as a person, that brings you very close to what drives them to strive for what they want to achieve and what makes them happy and fulfilled when they reach their goals.

That's why it's so important to get to understand someone's purpose. We can't devote every moment of our working lives to fulfilling our purpose; there's always some unexciting but important work that has to be done to get us to where we want to be, but if that work is taking us closer to our goals and toward fulfilling our purpose, then the work is energizing; it fills our emotional tanks.

Our purpose can change over the course of our careers, but in Michael's case I felt that was unlikely. "Working as a team to make a difference in people's lives" was what got Michael out of bed in the morning and kept him going, if necessary, through sixteen-hour working days.

Michael had been through a period of leadership shock for all the usual reasons: not because his purpose had changed but because the leadership style and the leadership behaviors that had stood him so well up until his appointment as CEO were suddenly not helping him achieve his new goals. In Michael's case, he was still trying to help and enable his colleagues and fix everyone's problems and keep everything running on track, when he needed to get clear of all those things and focus on big strategic goals. It's a common problem at that level of leadership.

But now that Michael had had the opportunity to stand back and reflect on his strengths, his vision, and his leadership approach, he had been able to reset his priorities and adapt his leadership style to the new challenge. He had achieved that metacognition we talked about earlier: the ability to reflect on your own thought processes and come to understand why you tend to do the things you do as a leader and decide whether that approach and those actions are the most appropriate and effective in your new leadership environment.

Once you have that ability to reflect on your leadership, you can use it to adjust it at will to cope with any future leadership challenges. Which is why you don't need Pete Steinberg anymore and why he experiences a period of mourning when your relationship comes to an end.

Having said that, clients do tend to stay in touch. They don't ring up and ask my advice, because they don't need to. But they often like to tell me about developments in their careers and, flatteringly, tell me how useful our work together has been for them.

I continued to work with Michael's company, helping with the development program for new leaders as the company expanded. I was able to watch the company grow as planned, with a series of dramatic acquisitions and expansion into new drug fields. I saw Kevin and Jimena settle very effectively into their roles. To be honest, I didn't get to see Michael much; I had no reason to walk into his office. Once in a while we would pass in the corridor and, if he noticed me, he would nod and smile.

And then, about four years after our work together, I saw the news that Michael had been appointed as CEO of one of the major pharmaceutical companies and would be taking up his role later in the year. It was a big deal. I was very happy for him. I sent him a quick note of congratulations by email and got a quick reply. I was expecting a nice, "Thanks Pete"—but there was more.

Dear Pete,

Thanks for your kind words. It's very exciting. Also a big challenge.

I wanted to say that there's hardly a day goes by when I don't reflect on my Authentic Leadership Model in some way. I think about whether I am devoting my time to the most important areas. I check what I am doing against my leadership principles: "Is this way of interacting with this colleague or this board member the best way to achieve my priorities and my vision?"

I have my copy of the leadership model in front of me as I type, and I'm already wondering what is going to change when I have a fuller understanding of the expectations of my new role and what should be my vision for the new organization's future.

So—thanks for all your earlier help. It was immensely valuable.

Keep up the good work!

With best wishes

Michael.

The company went through the usual period of soul-searching as it decided how to deal with Michael's departure, and I didn't get to hear much news from inside the organization: all leadership development programs were on hold during the transition period.

But then I got a phone call I wasn't expecting.

"Pete? Hi, it's Alicia."

"Alicia! How are you? How nice to hear from you!"

"I'm good. I'm er … Have you heard the news?"

I hadn't.

"Kevin's been made CEO. Jimena's leaving. She's landed a role as CEO of a really good rival outfit. I honestly don't know who would have gotten the role if it was a choice between Kevin and Jimena, but she'd been trying to decide whether to accept the role for a while—or so I understand, you know what I mean?"

I imagined there had been a few conversations over a few cocktails while Jimena and Alicia talked over Jimena's new opportunity.

"So, it's Kevin. And the new COO is ..."

She hesitated.

"The new COO is little old me. I've been in the role for a couple of months."

I started to tell her how delighted I was, and how much she deserved the role, and what a great COO she would be, but she cut me short.

"Yeh. The thing is ... It's my calendar, you know? It's out of control. I mean, I know all about the calendar thing, right? I saw what happened to Michael and I saw it get fixed. I just haven't been able to work out what's going wrong with mine. Nothing seems to be working right now. Everything's going *al infierno sobre ruedas.* And I think I am going literally insane. So, I was wondering ...?"

MARIA TAYLOR
CHIEF LEARNING OFFICER, UNITED AIRLINES

"Every Leadership Competency Model I've looked at looks pretty similar. They're all the same! I think, where you really need to triangulate is in what's needed. How would those leadership competencies translate into what's actually needed, by the goals of the business, by the environment, and by the audience? You know, executive presence and communication are both great examples. It's going to be very different, whether I'm giving a presentation to the board, or I'm talking to the union, or I'm speaking at a town hall. How do I keep true? Authenticity to me is, how do I keep true to my beliefs as a leader? How do I keep true to my goals as an organizational leader? And then how do I talk to people in a way that is empathetic and recognizes where they're coming from without being fake in any of it?

"I think we've been taught to value busyness and activity. But as a leader, as the person, you really need to take that step back. That's why things like meditation and resiliency training have taken hold. It's so important to reflect and step back and to look at, what's the impact of my actions? Am I directionally going the way I want to go? How do I even feel as a human being? I think, as we look at your personal values, if you don't understand what those are, and how those play out for you, you will make bad decisions. And having that center who you are ... it goes to how you treat people, what decisions you're willing to make, how you want to spend your time: percentage of time with business; percentage of time with family. Having that core value system and being cognizant of it is key."

Summary: Leadership Principles

The Authentic Leadership Model asks you to think about not just where you spend your time but also how you spend your time. Leadership principles help you focus on this.

The interesting thing about leadership principles is that they are not actions. They are not things that you decide you are going to do; they are principles you can hold yourself accountable to. There may be several different leadership actions you could take that would bring a principle to life.

Leadership principles come from your leadership beliefs and the value you provide, but they are also grounded in your purpose, vision, and priorities. They must be connected to the things you feel most deeply about: the goals you want to achieve and the things you believe will help you achieve those goals. This is the system in action—

different parts working and interacting with each other. Leveraging the system ensures that what you do as a leader continues to fill your emotional tank, makes you feel good about yourself, and gives you the energy to continue doing it.

Developing leadership principles can be one of the hardest things we do when I work with clients, but when we find the right principles, they are very powerful. As we saw in the last chapter, a good example of a leadership principle might be, "People will be empowered if they understand the strategy." This core principle might result in several different leadership behaviors, all of which stick to the core idea behind the principle, which is that the leader wants to empower the team to make their own decisions.

With that principle in place, a leader might always lead discussions based around strategic objectives; choose to pose questions to the senior team without supplying a ready answer; and set out clear boundaries about decision-making rights. They might choose to facilitate team members' thought processes as they make their own decisions, acting as a mentor for the team member rather than as a boss and demonstrating in practice that the decision is theirs to make. All these different leadership actions stem from the wish to encourage people to make their own decisions, encapsulated in the general principle of "People will be empowered if they understand the strategy."

As you develop your leadership principles, choose several potential principles and test them against your vision, your priorities, the value you bring, and your leadership beliefs. Then test them in the real world. It will likely take a few weeks before you can be certain that a leadership principle is getting you to where you want to be in your vision and helping you meet your priorities and, most importantly, that they lead to leadership behaviors that feel authentic.

Choosing Your Leadership Principles

Your leadership principles are the things that need to be true about your approach to leadership for you to be able to implement your priorities and your vision. This means they are principles that are true right now.

Leadership Principles:

- Define how you want to lead.
- Take the way you lead/think and make it explicit.
- Allow you to hold yourself accountable.

Developing your principles requires you to think about not only how you lead but also why you lead that way.

- Consider your *non-negotiables*.
- How do you *deal with challenges*?
- What is *important* to you about your *team*?

Be creative in developing your principles. A leadership principle should not begin with "I want." The right principle will guide your leadership behavior in every situation.

Good examples:

- "Top talent drives performance."
- "Open communication results in sharing best ideas."
- "Giving the team time to think enhances creativity."

EXERCISE:

Draw up a list of potential principles.

Test them against your vision, priorities, the value you bring, and your leadership beliefs.

Test them in the real world for a few weeks.

Are they helping you achieve your vision?

Are they leading to authentic leadership behaviors?

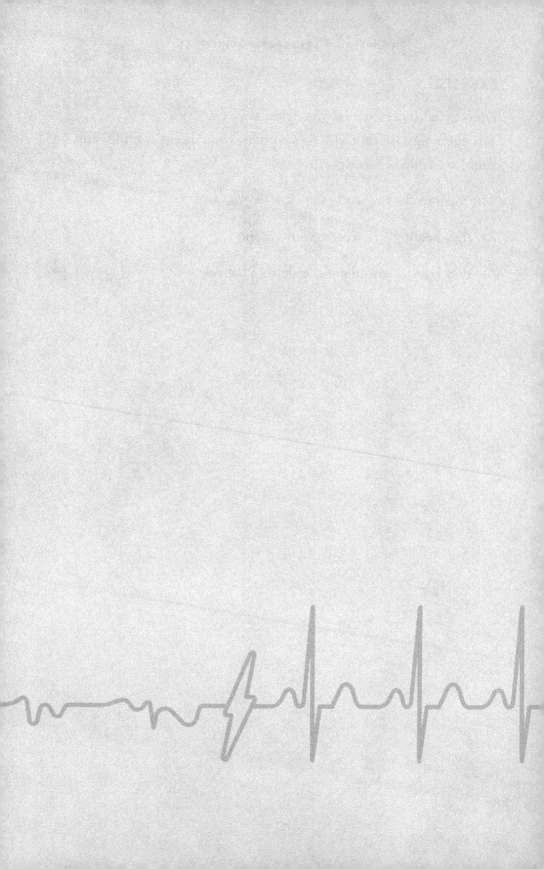

PAUL KONONOFF

PROFESSOR, UNIVERSITY OF NEBRASKA-LINCOLN

I'd like to introduce you to Paul Kononoff. Paul is a friend who also became a client.

I am going to use Paul's experience to illustrate the various aspects of the Authentic Leadership Model for several reasons: because he is pretty much a textbook example of leadership shock; because he has allowed me to share his story with you; and because he was skeptical about the whole idea of leadership shock and leadership coaching, which I feel helps to validate the model. If you're skeptical about something but you find it works after all, then we can be certain that "confirmation bias" isn't at play; you are not just persuading yourself that something is real, just because you want to believe it.

Paul works in academia—he is a professor at the University of Nebraska-Lincoln and, at the time, was a senior editor for the leading scientific journal in his field of dairy science. Paul had just been assigned the role of Editor in Chief for the journal.

Paul's background is probably very different from your own, but his experience in taking on a more senior role shows that leadership shock is universal. Leaders in every field have the same challenges and encounter the same problems—including leadership shock.

Paul, as you would guess, is a scientist at the top of his field. He had been a highly successful journal editor, just as he is a highly successful professor. He is the senior editor of the journal for articles that fall under his area of expertise. He reports to the Editor in Chief. The role of Editor in Chief for the journal is term-limited. One day, out of the blue, Paul received a call from the then-incumbent, who, as Paul tells it, said in effect, "Hey buddy; you're up." There was a process to the assignment and, once that had been followed, Paul was formally offered the role.

Paul accepted the role largely because he felt it was his duty to take it on and give something back to the journal and to the scientific community. He was completely confident in his ability to carry out the role successfully: he was a leading figure in his field; he enjoyed working with authors and discussing their research. The only downside to the editor's job was having to reject people's papers when they weren't up to the journal's standards or didn't pass the peer review system, but that was the name of the game. "Being a senior editor is not much different from being a professor," Paul told me. "It's about evaluating science and making decisions." The Editor in Chief's role, surely, would just be more of the same.

But then Paul found that, to his great surprise, it was not more of the same. Things didn't seem to be working anymore. Nobody else noticed and the journal continued to be successful, but Paul began to feel things were not under his control.

"What I realized," Paul said, "was that all the tools that I'd collected and put into my toolbox that had provided me with the success I have today … none of them were applicable. I felt like I was taking a fishing rod to a bear hunt. I'm a big systems guy, and I just felt like I had no system. I felt ill prepared. That maybe this wasn't even something I was cut out to be."

Sound familiar? Paul was experiencing leadership shock.

Paul had been a leader for many years—heading up a research program, giving advice and guidance, inspiring and motivating colleagues and students … but Paul's new role was different in some vital way. The old leadership model wasn't working, and suddenly everything seemed to be falling apart.

I should tell you that Paul and I go back a while. Paul was doing postgraduate work at Penn State University when I was head coach for the Penn State Women's Rugby team, and Paul was my assistant coach for four years or more. Paul is a great rugby player, a great coach, and a great leader.

Our careers later took us into very different worlds: academia, in Paul's case, and the world of executive coaching in my own case. And I discovered that Paul had a pretty dim view of my executive coaching world.

"I remembered the new stuff you were doing—the leadership coaching," Paul told me. "I always thought that was kind of just this hokey thing. I thought, 'Well, if I'm a good scientist and I'm a natural leader, I don't really need to go through these exercises.' So I was extremely skeptical. But I was getting to the point where my desperation was overcoming my skepticism."

He turned to me because he knew I was a good sports coach, which to Paul was a real thing as opposed to the hokey executive coaching thing, and he reached out, in his own words, out of desperation.

Yes: things were so bad that Paul had been forced to turn to his old friend "in desperation."

I'm happy to say that we are still friends and that the executive coaching thing worked very well for Paul. Let me tell you how our conversations went.

As we've seen throughout this book, I find that a useful place to start the conversation with any client is to ask when they feel best about themselves; when they feel most accomplished and comfortable, as if this is the thing they are meant to be doing. Because, in my experience, people generally feel best about themselves when what they are doing is closely aligned to what they believe in and what their purpose is.

Most of the time we give a quite simplistic account of what our purpose is in the context of our work. We talk about objectives and things we want to achieve—which are not the same as our purpose.

Our true purpose is something fundamental. It is what fills our emotional tank. It is what gets us out of bed in the morning excited to get started and allows us to go to bed at night feeling we have done something worthwhile. Asking people when they feel best about themselves is a very good way to reveal their true purpose.

But people's first answers to that question often don't quite get to the heart of the matter.

Paul's first answer was that he felt best when he was writing; that what he would most like would be to sit in his office at the university or back home in his study and focus while writing for long periods of time. Paul is a scientist, not a novelist, so what he meant by that was that he loved to write grants and scientific papers, which makes sense, because Paul is an academic and a thinker, and a big part of his function in life—his purpose—is to communicate ideas to other people. There is no point in being incredibly knowledgeable about something and discovering exciting new things through your research if you can't pass that on to other people.

But the more I talked with Paul about writing, the more I felt that there was something that lay behind the business of writing; something deeper. And, slowly, it became obvious that Paul loved to write because the act of writing helped him crystallize his thoughts. It forced him to assemble all his knowledge and put it down on paper in a form that other people could understand. We began to realize that Paul's chief purpose—the thing that made him feel best about himself—was learning and helping other people to learn, which should be obvious for someone who is a professor, but it came as a bit of a revelation to Paul and helped him greatly with the rest of the process of developing his leadership model.

Scientific journals are an absolutely vital part of the scientific process, allowing ideas to spread throughout the scientific community and be challenged and developed, and Paul was excited about learning more about the business of putting the journal together, and about scientific publishing in general. As he told me, "The thing you flushed out that has been particularly helpful to me—I can't believe I didn't realize it!—was that I'm really driven and motivated *to learn*."

Paul said that his insatiable curiosity had played a big part in accepting the role. It gave him a chance to learn about the mechanics of publishing and about how scientific journals are put together. What he had not properly taken into account was his visceral dislike of administration and business meetings.

But once Paul had realized that his *purpose* in his new role was to learn more about a field he had never explored before, the route to a new and effective leadership model opened up.

"That was critical for me," said Paul. "Just to come to grips with that, internally. Once I did, I could really follow through with the rest of the model."

So we did just that—we followed through with the rest of Paul's leadership model.

I would like to emphasize again at this point that the various inputs to the Authentic Leadership Model are not linear. You don't explore one aspect, then the next, then the next, and then the next to emerge at the end with the answer. They are all interconnected, and every aspect feeds into every other aspect. Something said late on in the process makes you revise everything that was said earlier.

I do always start with a leader's purpose, as we did with Paul. And Paul found, as always happens, that thinking about his core purpose—the thing that gets you out of bed in the morning and fills your emotional tank—helps to clarify a lot of other things. It helps to remind you of why, deep down, you are doing whatever it is you are doing right now; how you came to be here and why you do what you do. It is your fundamental intrinsic motivator.

The next thing we explore for the Authentic Leadership Model are the things that are specific to your current leadership role. At the heart of this is your vision for the role: what you want to achieve in the role and the things you need to make happen to know that you have been successful in the role.

In Paul's case, we found that he wasn't quite able to decide on his vision for his role until he had thought more deeply about another aspect of his leadership model: the value you bring to the role, which is, of course, closely related to the expectations of the role. It's not much use focusing on your great skills as an offensive tackle if you're being asked to play wide receiver—unless, of course, as is often the case, there is some fundamental value that you bring to both positions, some core strength you have as a skilled football player.

Let's talk about the value Paul brought to his role and the role expectations he faced, and then we will come back to his vision.

In Paul's case, the expectations for his role as Editor in Chief were many and various. In fact, there was an overwhelming formal list of expectations. The job descriptions that we all draw up for various roles are, intentionally, detailed and exhaustive. They help us identify the qualities that the ideal applicant for the role would have, and they give the successful applicant a precise account of their duties.

That is not the same thing as what the organization truly hopes you will achieve in the role. You will have to make sure that all the things listed in your job description get done, and get done very well, but there will actually be relatively few things that will define real success in the role.

One of Paul's problems—one which applies to many senior people—was that he didn't really have a formal "boss." He didn't have that one person that he reported to or who he could bounce ideas off of or ask for clear direction. He had a very long list of duties and obligations, but there wasn't any one person who could say, "This is what really matters; this is what we need you to achieve."

Paul's boss was accountable to the board, and the board was effectively the boss but Paul could not pin down a clear collective view of what they expected from Paul in his role as Editor in Chief.

Another of Paul's problems in his new role was that he was confused with his interactions with the board, because the board of the journal, quite understandably, had a wide range of interests that were not only about the advancement of scientific publishing but of other association activities.

"I'll be honest," Paul told me. "I would never be driven to sit on that kind of board. I'm interested in the science and the publishing, and then I realized I had to sit on this board, and I was confused with my role, my responsibilities, and my general understanding of how things worked."

At this point in my conversations with Paul, several important things began to coalesce.

I said to Paul that I thought the reason he was on the board of the journal was to ensure the well-being of the journal and that one of the key expectations of his role might be for him to represent the journal to the board and, in some instances, to serve to educate them about the operations and challenges the journal faces. He also needed to learn how to lean on them for feedback and support.

That was an important moment.

"That's not something that is written down anywhere," Paul told me. "But you're absolutely right." I remember clearly how animated Paul became. "It changes how I view the board," he said. "It's exciting. And I feel some important duties that come with that expectation."

This transformed Paul's view of board meetings. Instead of being a confused spectator, he began to see that his relationship to the board was meaningful and that he had a clear function on the board.

When we talked about the value that Paul brought to his new role, we focused on his knowledge—because Paul obviously brought a great deal of knowledge and wisdom to bear on the role—and his commitment. Paul is a conscientious man who felt a great sense of duty to bring all of his knowledge and skills to bear on the journal and contribute as much as he possibly could.

The other aspects of Paul's value were harder to tease out, simply because Paul genuinely doesn't like talking about himself or being the focus of attention. We slowly came to understand that a big part of Paul's value was that he was, as it were, "the real deal." He was completely authentic. And that was a great part of the value he brought to the role.

"I don't like talking in front of groups of people," Paul told me. "I mean, I can do it, but it's not something I gravitate to naturally. It's never been a strength of mine to manipulate words in front of people. Writing is OK. But speaking? No. But what I realized is that I could use this authenticity in working and leading people and leveraging items and groups of people toward my vision. I didn't think that was a strength of mine that I could use, but identifying that has been pretty liberating."

As Paul began to focus on the value he was able to bring to the role, the things that he wanted to achieve during his tenure—his vision—became clearer.

I asked Paul what he wanted the journal to look like in, say, three years' time; what he wanted key stakeholders, such as the board, the editors, and the wider scientific community, to say about his leadership.

After much time spent refining and whittling down his original list, Paul decided that there were two core things he wanted to achieve: to strengthen the reputation and worldwide influence of the journal and to help emerging scientists.

These two things can be unpacked into a wide range of other objectives, but they sum up perfectly what Paul hoped to achieve during his tenure. Everything that crossed his desk could now be easily and quickly assessed in terms of whether it made a significant contribution to achieving his vision or not.

"I thought there had to be a whole laundry list of things that I wanted to accomplish," Paul told me. "You get inundated with, 'Paul, you should do this, the journal should do this!' And all of a sudden, your list starts to grow. And that's where you start to feel overwhelmed; that's where I was early on. But now when these things cross my desk, it's easy. I realize 'OK, that fits in with my vision' or, 'No, that doesn't fit in with my vision.'"

It was around this point in our conversations that Paul, to his great surprise, found that my hokey leadership ideas were actually beginning to work for him. He was beginning to lose the feeling of being overwhelmed.

As our sessions began to draw to a close, we talked about Paul's approach to leadership. Paul, as I said, was very averse to the "charismatic leader" model of leadership. He didn't want to stand up and wave his arms around and persuade people to do things. What he wanted to do was, in his words, shepherd people toward a possible destination. And he had an absolute commitment to giving people the space and the freedom to have original ideas.

By this point, we had covered the key inputs to Paul's Authentic Leadership Model: his purpose and vision, the value he brings to the role, the expectations of the role, and his approach to leadership. The next stage of Paul's leadership model was the analysis of these inputs, because a deep understanding of each of those key aspects of your leadership model allows you to discover your real priorities and draw up a list of the leadership principles that will act as a benchmark for your behaviors.

A key power of the Authentic Leadership Model is its ability to clarify the things you should prioritize: the things that will help achieve your vision. Understanding your true priorities helps you to say "no" to some of the apparently infinite list of things you *could* be doing and to focus on the things that will actually move you closer to achieving your vision. To work like this, the leader needs a committed and capable team that is willing and able to pick up many of the small essential elements that must not be dropped but also do not require the leader to execute.

As Paul's leadership model began to take shape, Paul stopped doing some of the things that he could now see were nonessential. For example, he stopped running workshops for contributing authors as he had always done in the past. It was valuable, because it helped authors understand the standards of the journal and how best to present their work if they wanted it to be accepted. Paul enjoyed it, because it gave him a chance to meet other scientists and hear about their work. But it was something that the other senior editors could do, and Paul's time would be better spent elsewhere.

Having set his priorities, Paul was able to move on to choosing his guiding principles. These act as a guide to a leader's behavior in any given situation. As with your vision for your role, a good approach is to write down a long list of guiding principles that you believe are useful and true, but then select only the principles that best apply to your current role.

One of the most common causes of leadership shock is for leaders to apply some guiding principle that has proved very effective in their past careers but is not appropriate in their new role.

One of Paul's prior guiding principles had been to step in and personally help anyone who needed it: a struggling student perhaps or a colleague with a technical problem. Now he realized that he needed to step back; to absorb as much information as he could about the latest developments in his scientific field and then to make difficult editorial decisions about what was most significant and worthy of featuring in the journal.

One of Paul's new guiding principles was "Listening to everyone is a powerful tool in the community's journey." Another of his guiding principles became "Sacrificing volume in favor of quality ensures excellence and competitiveness." You can see Paul's representation of his Authentic Leadership Model at the end of the chapter.

My conversations with Paul were very satisfying. He came out of his leadership shock and emerged with a very clear idea of the unique qualities that he brought to his new role, of his authentic leadership approach and his vision for what he wanted to achieve in that role. Paul also felt that he had built the circuitry of an effective system he could rely upon and use.

I remember, in the early days, he described the often conflicting demands of his many constituents: authors; reviewers; editors; the board. "I just had all this swirling going on," Paul told me, "and I never felt I was making impactful steps forward."

By working together on Paul's leadership model, we were able to help him find the system that he needed to best leverage his unique strengths and his natural leadership style and to relate those to a new vision for his role.

We were able to focus on some areas that Paul was actually very good at, but which did not come entirely naturally to him. He became able to make a conscious decision to change some of his previous priorities and adopt new guiding principles that would best serve his new vision for what he wanted to achieve in the new role.

As Paul reflected on our time together, he said, "I remember saying to you, 'Pete, I need a system to work in, and I just can't find it.' And you said, 'Well, I'm about systems too.' And it made me think about our coaching days. You know, we had a game plan, so when players hit the field, when they're making decisions on where to kick the ball, where to pass the ball, they have the ability to think on their feet and think strategically.

"And you've helped match that game plan with who I am; with my authentic personality. Remember when you flushed out of me that I really enjoy training and working with editors? That's why I gave my leadership model the title, 'Diligent Learning and Steadfast Training.' That's very me."

Paul's Authentic Leadership Model

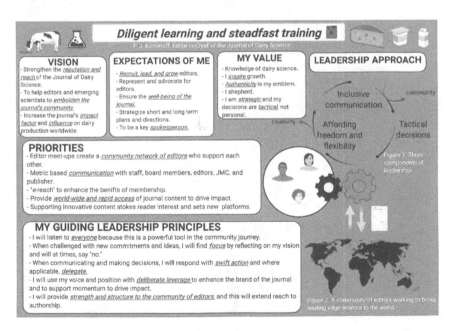

NICOLE MASSEY

VICE PRESIDENT OF MARKETING, CONSUMER FOODS DIVISION AT THE J.M. SMUCKER COMPANY

Nicole Massey was recently promoted to Vice President of Marketing, Consumer Foods Division at The J.M. Smucker Company. Nicole and I worked on her Authentic Leadership Model a few years ago. At that time, she was the director of food and beverage innovation for the company. We started by talking about her experience with the leadership model, and I asked her to define her role within her organization.

"Leading the development of innovation strategy," Nicole said, succinctly. "So, where our brands and our businesses are going to innovate and evolve; leading strategy development and ensuring that the teams are delivering against a pipeline of initiatives that will deliver against those business strategies and objectives.

"A key part of my role is about innovation in general, which is around helping the organization evolve: how we make decisions; how we can be more agile so that we are prepared for the future;

being a real engine for change. And that means that you're constantly trying to inspire the organization to do new things, which is not easy, because for most companies, fulfilling their business model is built on doing the same thing over and over again at scale. So you're constantly pushing up against what the organization likes to do or needs and wants to do every day. It requires tremendous relationship building, trust, and vision and the need to be able to inspire people to do things differently."

We talked about the concept of leadership shock. "Having experienced it a few times in my career, it's a very real issue," said Nicole. But when we started work on her Authentic Leadership Model, it was not leadership shock she was experiencing.

"I guess, for me, especially in my most recent experience, it was less about change and more about *intentionality*," she told me. "And maybe moving from working on instinct to operating with more intention. The process of documenting—putting on paper and articulating the elements of my Authentic Leadership Model—helped give me tools so that I could then be more deliberate and intentional about what I was doing and more focused with my time. It allowed me to be much smarter with my time and effort."

I asked Nicole about her experience of exploring her purpose as part of the work on her leadership model.

"It helped having to articulate it. It helps drive focus and choice. We all have a lot of different opportunities and a lot of different interests as we move through our lives and our careers. You have different interests and motivations at different times. None of us is solely laser focused on one purpose, or on one motivating force, I guess. But I do think that the exercise of articulating what my purpose was did help me zero in on what is the biggest, most important thing.

It allowed me to focus in, and then also articulate those things that are *not* my purpose.

"So, for my purpose, we agreed on: 'Drive lasting impact for the team, business, and consumers to make lives better.' Because you talk about what fills your bucket, right? What is it that makes you feel fulfilled at work. And for me, the things that make me feel fulfilled are: I want to have an impact; I want to have a meaningful role in positively impacting the business. But I also want to do it in a way that positively impacts the team and the people I work with, in ways that make their lives better. You can have an impact on the business and shred through people! So, to me, making lives better applies not just to consumers and making their lives better through convenient, consumer goods, but, truly, I want to have an impact on the work experience of my team, because I know that work experience has a huge impact on their life."

We talked about how we had explored Nicole's vision for her new role.

"I think this was a very helpful exercise because I was starting in a new role. And in my particular circumstance, the new role that I moved into was the type of role I had filled before, but in a smaller, more independent company, not something that was part of a much bigger conglomerate. I mean, it was a $3 billion company and now I'm in an $8 billion company, so, you know, they're still obviously both big! But there are meaningful differences in how an $8 billion company with three business units operates versus a $3 billion company with one business unit, where everyone's focused on the same thing. So, for me, it was a meaningful opportunity to stop and be deliberate about what I want to do with the team. How is my role potentially different in the context of this bigger company? And working through the time period. When you think about words like 'vision' and 'purpose,' they can feel so enormous and overwhelming. And I think focusing on, 'No, this is about the vision for the team in the next three to five years. What do I want to accomplish while I'm in this role?' is very helpful."

When we moved on to talk about our discussions regarding the expectations for Nicole's new role, we touched on how the role expectations are likely to be relatively flexible, that the organization may have a set of "basic" expectations for the role but that those expectations may be open for debate—especially more senior roles—and that a new leader may be expected to put their own stamp on those expectations.

"Talking about role expectations was a helpful exercise, because it gave me something of a launching pad for conversations with others in turn," Nicole said. "So I think, to your point, it's a pointless exercise if it takes place in a vacuum, because you can articulate what you think the expectations are, but there has to be a real conversation with the organization to make sure that they're aligned. I think there's also tension between the role expectation and any leader's ambition, in the sense that I think there's the baseline of what's expected and then there's, 'What does everyone hope that you can do with it, though? What is the ideal? What do *you* think you could do with it?'

"So the starting point for my role expectation was, 'Build and deliver an innovation pipeline for food and beverage.' Well, I'm the innovation director, so, obviously, I have to build and deliver an innovation pipeline! But there's a lot tapped into that, and under that, it isn't really fleshed out. So, in the context of the Authentic Leadership Model, I think it's helpful to articulate things that then have to be starting points for conversations with other people to really flesh out some more detail about my expectations and the organization's expectations. It's a very valuable part of process that I think is often side-stepped or forgotten. Also, 'Build and deliver an innovation pipeline' sounds very transactional. But there's a really important 'hearts and minds' aspect of innovation. It's not just about project management: come up with ideas and then project-manage them. It's about creating an atmosphere of safety where it's OK to innovate and take risks. That's what we want; that's the goal."

When we talked about how we had explored the value that Nicole brought to her new role, she talked again about the way the process had helped her focus on what she wanted to achieve in the role and the tool kit she had brought with her.

"There were a couple of things about reflecting on the value I bring. First, I think it helped me to go back to and think about the role expectations, and it gave me some inspiration to start to think about the 'how' and the 'what' of what I could accomplish: what I'm good at and where I can really add value. And second, because I was starting in a new role, and, in particular, one in which I didn't change levels but the span of control from a subject matter perspective had become very broad, I was overseeing two separate businesses and two separate teams. So, as a result, my time was stretched and I had to be much more thoughtful about where I engaged and where I could really make an impact and drive value; sitting down and really thinking about my tool kit, the value I provide. Where do I really employ them on my projects and my businesses? Is this a unique value that I can bring in or a way I can really have a big impact? And we decided the first is about experience with the process and that willingness to challenge the status quo. The second is being able to toggle quickly and easily between strategic and tactical thinking. The third is having and being able to build strong relationships. And the fourth is that I'm empathetic and adaptable."

When we came to talk about Nicole's leadership approach, she offered a good example of the way one's "natural" leadership style may not be appropriate in a new role or may simply be impractical. It may not be physically possible to operate with your previously preferred leadership style, for example, because of the time demands of the new role.

"Again, this wasn't so much about changing, because I was much more stretched, being much more intentional in my leadership approach. I believe a lot in coaching and teaching via an apprenticeship model, but that requires working side by side to some degree with the people on your team, and now I don't have the bandwidth to do that for every project and every person. Reflecting on that and articulating that allowed me to recognize that I have to be much more intentional and thoughtful. I think if I hadn't articulated this, I would have felt bad, because it would have felt like a gap to me. I would not have done what I would have instinctively felt was an important part of how I wanted to lead. But I realized that it wasn't possible to apprentice every team I have in every project. It allowed me to think. 'OK, so I'm going to do it here, here, and here' and recognize that that's probably where I am able to add the highest value and then be OK with the fact that I'm not doing it on every project."

I asked Nicole for her overall reflections on the process of working through her Authentic Leadership Model.

"Well, I would say I'm still early in the process of my new role. But to me it was about translating maybe instinct into just that much clearer, sharper articulation of leadership principles. I felt I knew I was a strong leader, but I don't think I could have articulated, until I sat down and really did this, the five or six things about my approach that make me effective and the things that are unique to me or things that I believe are important in terms of being a good leader.

"I will say, reflecting on the whole process, I was surprised when I started the process, because I don't know what I was expecting, but this is not what I was expecting. Maybe I was expecting to jump a bit more to the priorities? Maybe I was expecting to jump a bit to the approach to leadership? And it was really only once we got to perhaps our third session, where we start to talk about the value I bring and personal leadership … I think maybe that's where I was really getting into that, 'Oh, this is the doing part, right?' Which is how my brain works—I'm very much a 'doer.' But then I realized how valuable having the foundation of the first few sessions was. Having that foundational work, that input, makes sense of the approach to leadership and priorities. It gives you something to push those off and helps you decide on your trade-offs and priorities."

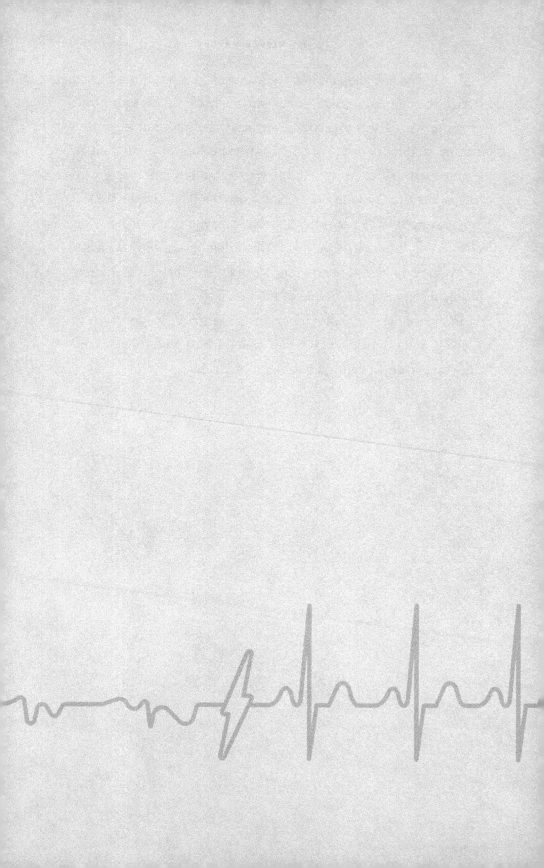

GEOFF TANNER

PRESIDENT AND CEO, SIMPLY GOOD FOODS

———

Geoff Tanner is currently President and Chief Executive Officer of Simply Good Foods, a $1.5 billion publicly traded nutritional snacking company. Prior to this appointment, Geoff was chief commercial and marketing officer for the $8 billion J.M. Smucker Company. He first joined Smucker in 2016 in a senior VP role when Smucker acquired the Big Heart Pet Brands, a pet food company backed by the private equity firms KKR, Vestar Capital, and Centerview Capital, where Geoff was VP marketing and general manager.

It was during Geoff's time at Big Heart Pet Brands that he and I worked together on his Authentic Leadership Model. Those were early days in my development of the model, and working with Geoff helped me develop the model to a new level.

We worked on all the elements of the model that I hope have become familiar to you in reading this book. Geoff's purpose at the time was crystal clear: "To help build a company that is recognized as one of the top companies in the world and is a household name. A place where our employees love coming to work and are proud to tell their friends and family they work there. This is what motivates me to come to work every day: to help build this place."

Geoff's vision was to build a company that made a difference in people's lives, and that delighted its consumers with amazing products and experiences and its investors with sustainable, profitable growth. Geoff was committed to his concept of Total Innovation: dealing with a rapidly evolving market environment through constant innovation and the ability and willingness to pivot strategically when required. He talked about the "art and science" of innovation: being grounded in data, insights, and testing, but also using intuition, judgment, and design to create great customer experiences.

Geoff's commitment to innovation led him toward a particular approach to leadership. He put great emphasis on honesty between team members—being able to tell the truth to each other and embrace dissent—and having the courage to take risks, question the status quo, and try new things. He embraced hypothesis-driven decision-making, which was then debated and tested. He said that he, as leader, would always speak with conviction, but that didn't mean that he was always right. He asked the team to debate and challenge and he believed that in order to do that, he had to encourage and protect divergent points of view.

You won't be surprised to learn that Geoff was, and is, a highly successful business leader. He achieved great things at Big Heart Pet Brands. The initial plan had been to take the company public with an Initial Public Offering (IPO). When The J.M. Smucker Company acquired the company instead, Geoff thought it was time to take a well-earned break. Instead, Smucker's General Manager and soon-to-be CEO, Mark Smucker, invited Geoff to join the executive leadership team at Smucker—the first time an outside person had joined the executive leadership team in the company's one-hundred-plus-year history.

We're going to hear Geoff's story in his own words in just a moment. I think I had better issue a spoiler alert at this point: his story is all about leadership shock. Geoff found that the corporate culture of the Ohio-based Smucker Company was very different from the private-equity-backed, hard-driving corporate culture he had most recently experienced in San Francisco. He quickly found that his established management style was not welcomed, to put it mildly, and that he was seen as an "outsider" who had come in to force through unwelcome change. As he puts it, he failed "to lead with empathy and show up as my full self."

I'll let Geoff tell his own story. The key lesson from Geoff's experience is that working through your Authentic Leadership Model provides a framework that will always allow you to adapt to a changed leadership environment but—and this is crucially important—any individual leadership model itself becomes outdated the moment it is created, because circumstances, environments, and challenges immediately begin to change. The leadership model as it is written down encapsulates the current challenges, the most important values you bring to the role, your current priorities, and the leadership style you believe is most appropriate to the role at that moment in time. The *framework* of the Authentic Leadership Model will allow you to adopt the *content* of the model to every new leadership challenge.

Geoff is a highly thoughtful leader and, like every successful leader, his success made him feel immune to leadership shock. As Geoff told me—and as you will see in the following pages—his first reaction to his new appointment at J.M. Smucker was, "All right, well, you know, I've done this before; no problem."

But that wasn't how things turned out ....

Geoff and I spoke in early 2021 about his career, his experience of leadership shock, and our time working together and about his approach to authentic leadership.

"I would say my most significant experience of leadership shock happened about six years ago," Geoff told me. "I was working for a company in the pet food sector. We had split from Del Monte, where I had worked for several years, and we were based in San Francisco and owned by private equity. We were a two-and-a-half-billion-dollar company, and I was vice president marketing and general manager. This would have been back in about 2015. I reported to the CEO, and the plan was that we were going to likely IPO the company, and I was being mentored by him. Then, a little bit out of the blue, we were acquired by The J.M. Smucker Company, which is a Fortune 500 company based out of Orrville, Ohio, that has been run by the Smucker family for over a hundred years. Very Midwest, very traditional. And I was thinking, 'Oh, well, we were going to IPO, now we're not. Perfect time for a sabbatical!' I had it all mapped out. Our kids were two and zero. And I was thinking, 'What a great time to do this. They're not going to school or anything; we could all just go on a trip and take a break!'

"So the company had been acquired, and The Smucker Company was doing an investor day in New York at the Stock Exchange, and I had to go out there and talk about the business they had purchased. When I was there, I met Mark Smucker, who was then the general manager of the company and next in line to be CEO. He asked if we could meet up later in a bar in New York, and I said, 'Sure!' You know:

'You're the boss!' And over a beer he told me he was going to be made CEO in six months, which was a lot earlier than anyone thought, and he was forming a new executive leadership team, and he asked me if I would be interested in joining the team.

"I knew at that point that it was a job offer that was probably too good to turn down. I was forty-one, and here I was being offered a job in the C-suite of a Fortune 500 company. We didn't initially want to move to Ohio, but we got our heads around that, and we moved. And I was super excited to be on the C-suite of a Fortune 500 … the sort of thing that you dream of. 'This is going to be great!' It had happened five or ten years sooner than I thought it would, and that was great.

"So we moved to Ohio. The company needed to transform itself, and that was the reason why Mark was becoming CEO. And one of the reasons why he asked me to take this role was to spearhead that transformation. And I was thinking, 'All right, I've done this before; no problem.' What you do is you put a phone call in to McKinsey or another major consultancy and you formulate a strategy, and then you jump in and start working on some big ideas, really get that going. And then, you know, 'I'll really drive hard, like I did when I was with the PE-backed company in San Francisco. So I've got this.' And I think that's the challenge—whenever you show up, you are predisposed to run the playbook that you ran prior. And I think that's what gets you in trouble.

"So I started off doing that, and things started to go bad very quickly. There's a whole slew of things that were working against me. Firstly, a lot of people just didn't think I deserved the job, coming in from the outside. I think I was the first outside corporate officer that was ever appointed at Smucker, because this was a place that didn't typically recruit from the outside. And then at that time I wasn't actually running the businesses, but I was charged with helping change how they were being run, which is a pretty challenging position to be in: not in a line-management role but charged with fundamentally changing how each business goes to market. And some of the people weren't exactly happy to see me show up.

"I'd grown up in a world where you didn't really talk about your family or your life or anything at work, you just went in and did your job. And this was an American Midwest company where it's family first, people first; business second. A massive culture change, which I was oblivious to. And it was also a culture that, at that time, was extremely fragile, that had just acquired this large business that I was part of. There was some bad blood during the integration. We were a San Francisco business, and this was a business based in Orrville, Ohio, and I think a lot of assumptions were made on both sides that weren't healthy.

"By the time I showed up, there was understandable tension between the two operations. I always describe it as, in a way, there were a couple of bullets looking for a target. When I left San Francisco for Orrville, the people in San Francisco were like, 'You sold out! You took the big job and you sold out!' And when I showed up in Orrville, the people in Orrville were like, 'Finally, we have a target!' It was a really difficult period. I also wasn't doing myself any favors because I just wasn't leading well at all. I describe it as 50 percent situational and 50 percent my own lack of being equipped to lead with empathy and show up as my full self and not as this sort of corporate … you know?

"So, anyhow, I showed up, and very quickly, things went pretty bad. I was sure I was going to get fired. I can remember checking my employment contract at least twice. It took a toll physically. I had permanent headaches. When you walk into your place of work every day and know that people don't want you there, it's horrible. So that was a situation I stepped into, and I was sure I was going to get fired, or at least a 50 percent chance, just because of how many people wanted me out.

"My boss, the CEO, Mark, took me aside and gave me some very difficult feedback. HR had been involved, and I went home that night and didn't really sleep. I was thinking, 'Oh God, I'm not leading with resonance; I'm constantly challenging and driving; not spending time with people to get to know them as people first.' It was very difficult. You go through life, you have your ups and downs in your career, but you don't often expect to hit a wall like that. So I came home and I didn't sleep, and I decided on a couple of things.

"One that I need to treat this as a learning opportunity, because a lot of the feedback was right. It's right, and I'm not leading as the kind of leader I would want to be. You know, I'm with my kids and being silly and funny, I play the piano, I do all this stuff at home, but then I get in the car, show up at work, and, too often, out jumps the hard-driving, 'business, business, business' leader! And deep down I knew that this was not the way to inspire people and deliver the change we needed. But I was acting a little on muscle memory. And that's a common thing—I see that a lot with people in new roles—muscle memory takes over. And I was like, 'You know what? I want to use this opportunity to really reorient myself as a leader. Because when I stared the feedback in the face, I was thinking, 'I don't want to be that person and there's got to be a different way. I'm going to try to use this, where I am right now, to figure it out.'

"And so I was just very intentional, and I was stubborn about working and learning to become a better leader. Now—and this is important—it would have been very easy to totally pivot and swing hard the other way, toward popularity. But a coach reminded me, 'Geoff, don't ever forget why they brought you here. They brought you here to change the company, so don't ever forget that.' Because you could easily forget that; you could just decide, 'You know what, my job is to be popular.' No, it's not. My job was to lead with resonance to inspire and then drive the change we needed.

"I went on this journey of, 'I need to change the way I'm leading without losing what I'm here to do.' And, honestly, it was a phenomenal experience, because it totally changed me as a leader. Completely. But here's the thing: it changed me as a leader, but it did not change me as a person. Because I decided, I'm just going to lead with absolute integrity to who I am as a person. I'm not going to try to be anything I'm not, I'm just going to be the same person I am at home and in other parts of my life. I'm just going to be that way at work too. And there's lots of aspects to that. If I don't think I've got the answer to something, I don't mind admitting it. I'll make fun of myself when it's deserved. I want to know people as people. I'm not going to start every meeting with, 'Tell me about your top KPIs,' but rather, 'What did you do on the weekend? How's the family?' Manage as a human. Lead as me.

"I wanted to break down that barrier that exists between me as a person and me as a business leader. Like I said, I play the piano so I performed several concerts at work and invited employees on stage to sing. My kids came to work often. I held the divisional holiday party at my house, where my kids and their friends helped out. And along the way, people maybe began to think, 'Oh, he's not a bad guy, you know?' I tried to never lose sight of why I was brought into Smucker and kept driving more and more change, but it was just done very differently. Instead of, 'What's the strategic plan? Let's call McKinsey!' Or you know, 'Let's call IDEO, the design firm, let's have their project plan!' It was, 'Let's be human: a human being first; a father; a friend. And then we'll do stuff together to get the business on the right path.' And that was sort of the show.

"And in the time since that happened, I picked up more responsibility and became the chief commercial and marketing officer. We led a massive transformation of how we went to market. We drove substantial market share gains (from 25 percent of the portfolio growing or maintaining share to greater than 75 percent) and we saw significant stock price appreciation (from $93 to $160). *Fast Company* magazine even listed us as one of the most innovative companies in the world. Equally importantly, we developed some phenomenal talent and leaders. And this was all built on a leadership unlock which is, 'I'm going to bring my whole self to work. And if you like it, you like it, and if you don't, at least you know you're getting the real me and it's not just some corporate game I'm playing.'"

Geoff had been through a severe episode of leadership shock, but he had been able to use the framework of the Authentic Leadership Model and recognize that his earlier approach to leadership was no longer appropriate in the new environment and that he needed to revisit that approach and his leadership principles.

I asked Geoff about the vision he had for Smucker at that time.

"I always had a strong sense of our vision and opportunity as a company. This is obviously critical. And I've always had a relentless drive (it drives my wife Catherine crazy!) but there was no way I was going to lead, inspire, and help a large group get there with the leadership mindset I showed up with. The only way to get there is to be authentic, real, genuine, honest, open, and vulnerable. Some of the things that you may have been taught are not appropriate in leadership. But people follow people. Knowing roughly where you want to go is important. And knowing what your role is. Your job is not to do the work; your job is to help others do the work. And then I think your job is to make sure you have the absolute best people you can; I couldn't underscore that enough. Your job is to remove obstacles and enable them. Underpinning it all is ensuring that there's accountability. People have to be held accountable. People want to be held accountable. When they see others not held accountable, they don't like it.

"Another thing: lead with full transparency. When you ask people how the results are going, they just spin it. I'm not going to spin it; I'm going to tell it like it is. We'll face the brutal facts together, and I'm not going to sugarcoat it. If it's good, it's good; if it's not, it's not."

I asked Geoff about how he made decisions about whether to operate as a hands-off leader or to get personally involved.

"I think it's partly intuitive," he said. "I think where you know you've got good people, you tend to back off and where you know it's not your area, you tend to delegate a bit more. One of my weaknesses is systems and processes and that kind of stuff ... just not my strength. So if I have a strong leader in that area and the risk is low, I tend to back off a bit. In contrast, we might have something going on with Walmart or Amazon, and there's a meeting, and it's a strength of mine to be in front of a customer, and it's our largest customer, and if it goes wrong, you know ...

"I have watched many leaders say they are all about empowerment, and they sit back and don't really engage. Your job as a leader is to still add value. Yes, first and foremost you have to manage people, but at times you have to be on the field too. I've watched people say, 'Oh, I'm an empowering leader,' and as far as I can tell, they're really not doing anything. And it's pretty easy for those people to hide in large corporations. To your point, you can't do everything. But I do think you have a responsibility to be driving value.

"Other areas like brand building, marketing, innovation, and also the financial side—this is my wheelhouse, so I will probably show up more there. I do a quick calculus of, 'What's the impact to the business? How good is the person in the role? Where can I add value?' If it's an area that's more in my swing zone, I'll engage a bit more. Now to be clear, I still want to stay close to and on top of the total business, I just go a little deeper where I think I can add value."

Finally, I asked Geoff what two or three things he had wanted to achieve during his time at the company that did not have numbers attached to them and were more about corporate culture.

"There's a couple of angles to it. One is, culturally, I really wanted to build a place where everyone feels they belong and can be fully open, fully transparent. Where they feel free to speak up and challenge, to be as close to a democracy and meritocracy as you can get. Because it's only then that the best ideas will rise up, and the stupid ideas will be killed off. That's one thing. And that means people need to genuinely feel they can challenge me. And I love it! The second thing was that I wanted us to become much more diverse as an organization in the composition of leaders and how we think. And then thirdly, I think, more and more people need to start drawing a larger circle around what it means to be a leader. Large companies exist in society. They're not divorced from it, they're in it. And if you're in it, and if you're selling your product to society, and if you take a step back and see inequity and injustice in that society, but you say, 'Oh, it's someone else's problem,' you are making the choice not to lead. I'd love to see more people recognize that leadership doesn't end with the narrow description of their job and delivering a number. It's just expanding that circle of leadership to say, 'Well, I don't think it's enough to be a corporate leader.' I think if you're occupying a position at a senior level, in a large corporation, you have to be a leader in the community and in society at large.

"I'm not talking about 'The company has a philanthropic arm,' I'm talking about you individually as a leader. I believe as leaders we need to draw that circle wider and wider. And right now, I'm drawing it to also include personal leadership in the community, particularly to help underprivileged groups. For example, I formed a charity in Ohio, in partnership with the Boys and Girls Clubs, that provides music education access and inspiration to over ten thousand kids. It's called Opening Track. We worked with the Rock & Roll Hall of Fame, Cleveland Symphony, Playhouse Square, and others plus the local sports teams, Browns, Cavs, and Guardians, to develop and deliver a multifaceted program. The influence and impact you can have as a senior business leader is significant. We raised a lot of money and when I called these partner organizations, they picked up the phone and asked how they could help. This is leadership with a wider circle. Honestly it was as rewarding for me and my family as I think it was with the kids. My experience during that time was a rapid awakening. People want to work with people that are authentic, kind, and compassionate and I think increasingly that means drawing a wider leadership circle and being conscious and 'paying back' some of the advantages and breaks that got you here."

Printed in the USA
CPSIA information can be obtained
at www.ICGtesting.com
JSHW021535160324
59324JS00002B/2